# THE GREAT COMMISSION

## Models of Evangelization in American Catholicism

### TIMOTHY E. BYERLEY, PhD

Paulist Press
New York/Mahwah, NJ

The study questions for this book are available at www.paulistpress.com.

The cover artwork, "Absolution Under Fire" by Paul Wood (1891), has been reproduced with the permission of the Snite Museum of Art, University of Notre Dame, Notre Dame, IN.

IMPRIMATUR +
Most Reverend Joseph A. Galante, DD, JCJ
Bishop of Camden
August 3, 2007

Cover design by Lynn Else
Book design by Sharyn Banks

Library of Congress Cataloging-in-Publication Data

Byerley, Timothy E.
    The great commission : models of evangelization in American Catholicism    /
Timothy E. Byerley.
        p. cm.
    Includes bibliographical references (p.        ).
    ISBN 978-0-8091-4558-4 (alk. paper)
    1. Catholic Church—Missions—United States. 2. Missions—Theory. I. Title.
    BV2190.B94 2008
    266'.273—dc22

                                                                        2008011661

Published by Paulist Press
997 Macarthur Boulevard
Mahwah, New Jersey 07430

www.paulistpress.com

Printed and bound in the United States of America

# TABLE OF CONTENTS

Table of Contents

In loving memory of
my mother,
Joan B. Byerley

# ACKNOWLEDGMENTS

This book began as a doctoral dissertation at Fordham University's Graduate School of Religious Education under the supervision of Dr. John Elias, Fr. German Martinez, and Msgr. Thomas Shelley. I am grateful for their guidance and advice, especially in the first drafts of the work.

One of the high points of my experience at Fordham was coming to know Avery Cardinal Dulles. I thank the cardinal for his gracious counsel in the development of the manuscript and for writing the foreword for this book.

In the process of transforming the dissertation into a version suitable for general readership, I am indebted to my brother Fr. Joseph Byerley for his contributions. He is a great brother and a great priest. I am also most grateful to Alexander Marchione and his wife Caren for the efforts they expended in reviewing the text. Their input and suggestions were invaluable.

I also wish to thank Genevieve Deichert and her daughter Laura for the typing and technical refinement of the manuscript at every stage of its development.

Finally, I wish to express my gratitude to my father Edward, my brother Curt, my sister-in-law Joanie, and my nieces Katie and Kristen for their constant love and support in my priestly ministry.

# FOREWORD

From the time of Vatican II, and especially in the last quarter of the twentieth century, the popes have been urging Catholics to engage more vigorously in evangelization. Two landmark documents along this road were Paul VI's apostolic exhortation *Evangelii Nuntiandi* (1975) and John Paul II's encyclical *Redemptoris Missio* (1990).

In the United States, and perhaps elsewhere, the reaction to these initiatives has been disappointing. The statistics gathered by Nancy Ammerman in her 2005 book, *Pillars of Faith,* are illustrative. Asked whether spreading the faith was a high priority of their parishes, 75 percent of conservative Protestant congregations and 57 percent of African American congregations responded affirmatively, whereas only 6 percent of Catholic parishes did the same. Asked whether they sponsored local evangelistic activities, 39 percent of conservative Protestant congregations and 16 percent of African American congregations responded positively as compared with only 3 percent of Catholic parishes.[1] Converts to Catholicism often report that on their spiritual journey they received little or no encouragement from Catholic clergy whom they consulted.

The causes of this Catholic reluctance are complex, and would be difficult to summarize in a few sentences. My own experience is that Catholics before Vatican II were much more zealous in spreading the faith than they are today. In spite of the strongly affirmative statements in the *Dogmatic Constitution on the Church* and the *Decree on the Church's Missionary Activity,* the council has often been interpreted as if it had discouraged evangelization. Yet Paul VI, who was highly qualified to judge the intentions of the council, declared that its primary objective was "to make the Church of the twentieth century ever better fitted for proclaiming the Gospel to the people of the twentieth century" (*Evangelii Nuntiandi,* no. 2). John

Paul II likewise declared that Vatican II sought to renew the Church's missionary activity and that the recent decline of the missionary spirit in some sectors was by no means in accord with the directives of the council (*Redemptoris Missio,* nos. 1–2). These popes clearly taught that a healthy ecumenism and a readiness to acknowledge all that is good and true in non-Christian religions should not interfere with the Church's mission to proclaim the fullness of the gospel everywhere and to all.

In the American context, many Catholics have failed to grasp the Church's concept of evangelization, as taught by Vatican II and the recent popes. They confuse it with certain practices of sectarian Protestants, who use very aggressive tactics and seem satisfied to generate a subjective experience of having been saved by the Lord. Paul VI, however, defined evangelization in much broader terms, as "the grace and vocation proper to the Church, her deepest identity." He went on to say: "She exists in order to evangelize—that is to say, in order to preach and teach, to be the channel of the gift of grace, to reconcile sinners with God, and to perpetuate Christ's sacrifice in the Mass, which is the memorial of his death and Resurrection" (*Evangelii Nuntiandi,* no. 14).

Fr. Timothy Byerley, a priest of the Diocese of Camden, New Jersey, is well equipped by training and experience to clarify and promote the Catholic view of evangelization, as he does in the present book. He is the pastor of a parish, a scholar with a doctorate in religious education, and the co-founder and director of the Collegium Center for Faith and Culture, based in Deptford, New Jersey, which conducts various works of Catholic evangelization.

From his extensive knowledge of the New Testament and American Church history, Byerley distills six models or styles of evangelization. He does not claim that these six are the only models that could be named, but in my judgment they cover the field quite adequately. In order to supplement and confirm his analysis, which gives many interesting and informative examples, I should like to suggest some additional examples from universal Church history.

The first of Byerley's models, the witness of a life totally dedicated to the faith, has often proved very effective. St. Paul seems to have been greatly moved by witnessing the death of the Church's first martyr, St. Stephen. There can be no doubt that the example of the early martyrs in the Roman Empire made a deep impression on the minds of many pagan observers. These martyrs bore admirable witness to the strength of their conviction, to the ardor of their hope, and to the power of grace to sustain them in their trials.

Personal witness can also occur on much less dramatic levels. I recall reading a brief statement by Walker Percy on his reasons for becoming a Catholic. He mentioned particularly the example of a college classmate who used to steal off quietly to Mass every morning without speaking to others about the importance of faith. His devotion was a kind of silent sermon, deeply affecting the young Percy.

As a second model, Byerley proposes worship. In that connection I am reminded of the experience of John Henry Newman. During his years as a leader of the Oxford Movement in the Church of England, he was haunted by the fear that he and his friends were defending a "paper church"—one that existed in the writings of theologians but had no living congregations behind it. On his voyage to Italy and especially to Sicily in 1833, he was impressed by the crowds devoutly attending Mass and raising their voices in hymns to God. Without yet being persuaded of the truth of Catholic doctrine, he came to a realization that the Church of Rome was capable of arousing "feelings of awe, mystery, tenderness, reverence, devotedness, and other feelings which may especially be called Catholic."[2] The pious worshipers who so impressed Newman had no realization that they were engaged in evangelization; they would surely have been surprised to be told of their part in the conversion of the most celebrated theologian of his time in England.

The third model consists of verbal testimony: proclamation and catechesis. Any number of great missionaries, beginning with St. Paul, could be mentioned in this connection. St. Francis Xavier was outstanding. He not only preached to great masses of infidels; he assiduously catechized young and uninstructed converts in the elements of the faith. More than this, he engaged in disputations with learned bonzes in Japan, answering their difficulties and objections. With the ardor of his faith and the warmth of his charity, Xavier was able to reach children and illiterate audiences, but he was also equipped to contend with scholarly adversaries, drawing on his studies in philosophy and theology at the University of Paris.

As his fourth model for evangelization, Byerley speaks of communities of committed believers. In some of my own reading I have been struck by the power of attraction exercised by such communities. The sociologist Rodney Stark, in his historical study *The Rise of Christianity,* concludes that Christianity grew because "Christians constituted an intense community, able to generate the 'invincible obstinacy' that so offended the young Pliny but yielded immense rewards. And the primary means of its growth was through the united and motivated efforts of the growing numbers of Christian believers, who invited their friends, relatives, and neighbors to share 'the good news.'"[3]

Byerley's fifth model, inculturation, could be illustrated by many examples. Much has been written of the work of Matteo Ricci in China and Robert de Nobili in India. These two seventeenth-century Jesuits, among others, boldly adapted Catholic Christianity to the highly developed cultures of Asia. John Paul II published in 1985 a remarkable encyclical, *Slavorum Apostoli,* on the work of Sts. Cyril and Methodius, two blood brothers from Greece whose missionary efforts in and about Dalmatia embedded the faith in several Slavic languages and cultures, enabling the peoples of those lands to make a specific contribution to the catholicity of the Church. Thanks in great part to these great missionaries, the Church of the first millennium was able, as John Paul II puts it, to breathe with both lungs, Roman and Byzantine.

Finally, Byerley comments on the evangelistic power of works of charity, his sixth model. Benedict XVI, in his encyclical *Deus Caritas Est,* reminds us that the emperor Julian the Apostate regarded the Church's charitable activity as the chief reason for the popularity of the "Galileans" in the fourth century. Julian, in a spirit of competition, strove to make similar good works a feature of his restored paganism (*Deus Caritas Est,* no. 24). Within recent memory we have seen how Dorothy Day in New York and Blessed Teresa of Calcutta drew many to the faith by their ministry of charity to persons in need, serving them without regard to their religious affiliation.

Byerley's book gives a solid biblical basis to each of the six models. Writing primarily for American readers, he then gives interesting historical examples from our own national history, with which most American Catholics are all too unfamiliar. But he does not let his discussion end with evocations of the past. He invites the reader to reflect on the present value of each model and its pertinence to religious education. His objective is not only to inform the mind but also to inspire the will and indicate fruitful lines of action. His book will undoubtedly help many readers to find modes and styles of evangelization well suited to their abilities and situations. Too many refrain from evangelization because they have narrow or distorted concepts of what the term involves.

Byerley is sensitive to the fact that in speaking of evangelization he is dealing with a mystery of grace. The evangelist, however energetic and skillful he or she may be, is powerless to accomplish anything without the grace of God. As St. Paul wrote to the Corinthians, "I planted, Apollos watered, but God gave the growth. So neither he who plants nor he who waters is anything, but only God who gives the growth" (1 Cor 3:6–7). And yet all who engage in the process of spreading the gospel have the inestimable privilege of being what St. Paul calls "fellow workers of God" (1 Cor 3:9). We cannot use the primacy of God's grace to excuse us from doing our part, according to our particular calling. In giving us the faith, God gives us a commission to share it. Because much has been given to us, much will be required of us. We must not let our talents go unused.

The Church today is confronted with apostles of de-Christianization who are using all the available media to undermine and uproot Christian faith. In so doing these adversaries are not only imperiling the salvation of souls; they are debasing the moral and religious standards that have sustained our civilization in past centuries. They are weakening the bonds of universal charity that alone holds forth the promise of peace among nations.

The rebirth of evangelization for which the popes have been calling is desperately needed. The present volume, I believe, is ideally suited to meet this need. Informative, attractively written, and spiritually nourishing, it lends itself equally to private reading and to use in classes or discussion groups. It deserves a broad readership for many years to come.

*Avery Cardinal Dulles, SJ*
Laurence J. McGinley Professor of Religion and Society
Fordham University
Bronx, New York

# INTRODUCTION

*We wish to confirm once more that the task of evangelizing all people constitutes the essential mission of the Church.*

—*Paul VI*[1]

From the moment Jesus charged his disciples with the Great Commission—to *go into the whole world and proclaim the gospel* (Mk 16:15) — the mission of spreading the gospel has taken many forms. Of these various forms, there are six standard patterns that emerge throughout Church history as primary models of Christian evangelization. They are derived from the New Testament and represent the perennial paradigms of the Church's missionary activity.

This work identifies, defines, and evaluates these models of evangelization and describes their salient features. In order to help the reader grasp the models, I have included a corresponding example from American Church history to illustrate each of them. A concrete example is often more indicative of a model than a dry theological explanation, and also more revelatory of the inspiration and motivation that undergirds the work of evangelization. There are great moments of evangelical fervor in the American Catholic experience that illustrate the biblical paradigms quite effectively.

The purpose of this study is to highlight and promote the apostolate of evangelization and thus help to clarify and stimulate this essential mission of the Church. The positing of six primary models of evangelization can add a unique perspective to the current discussion of this important topic. A practical theology of mission that takes into account today's pluralistic circumstances while remaining faithful to the New Testament tradition will certainly contribute to the Church's recognition of her responsibility to bring the message of Christ to every person. I hope that this work will enlighten, encourage, and perhaps even inspire clergy and lay leaders with a renewed understanding and appreciation for the evangelical dimension that must be a part of all Church ministry today.

## Overview of the Study

The study begins with this introduction, which explains the nature and importance of evangelization. The main body of the book follows, which consists of six chapters. Each chapter presents one of the New Testament models of evangelization with an accompanying example and some considerations for religious education. The models, as I have identified them, are the St. Stephen model, the Jerusalem model, the Proclamation model, the Fraternity model, the Areopagus model, and the Loaves and Fishes model.

The St. Stephen model is based on Acts 7:54–60, which records the martyrdom of St. Stephen. It demonstrates the overwhelming power of Christian witness as a testimony to the gospel. All other forms of evangelization are effective to the degree that the evangelists are living icons of Christ. The example chosen from American history to illustrate the St. Stephen model is the Jesuit mission to the Native Americans from 1632 to 1672.

The Jerusalem model reveals the power of the Church's liturgical life, especially the Eucharist, to bring people to Christ. Acts 2:42, 46a, 47 relates how the early Christians gathered together and celebrated the Eucharist. This sacramental worship has always been mission oriented and by its very nature has attracted others to Jesus. The liturgy was used by Blessed Junipero Serra (1713–84) and his fellow Franciscans in the Spanish missions to the California Native Americans from 1769 to 1833.

The Proclamation model of evangelization is the verbal announcement of the gospel. This proclamation of Christ's message also includes education in the faith that leads to Christian maturity. This is the mode of promoting the gospel that is most often viewed as evangelization. St. Peter's discourse after Pentecost (Acts 2:14–41) is the first recorded account of this method of evangelization in Church history. An excellent example of this model in American history is the parish mission crusade, which reached its peak between 1830 and 1900.

In the Fraternity model a small community, or more properly, a core group of devoted, well-trained disciples, is formed and sent forth to evangelize. This was the method the Lord himself used to spread the gospel to the ends of the Earth. Mark 3:13–19 recounts Jesus' calling, forming, empowering, and commissioning his apostles. This group of twelve constituted the evangelical nucleus that propagated the message of salvation throughout the entire Roman Empire and beyond. The Fraternity model highlights the importance of small, well-formed communities in carrying out the Church's mission of evangelization. An inspiring example of the Fraternity model in American history is the Missionary Society of Saint Paul the Apostle, founded by Fr. Isaac Hecker in 1858.

The Areopagus model depicts the effort to transform every stratum of a given culture or people into a Christ-centered society. It claims St. Paul's discourse at the Areopagus as its prototype. St. Paul's apology in Acts 17:16–34 is considered the paradigm of the encounter of the gospel with human culture. This speech to the Athenians is the first word in the centuries-long dialectic between Christ and Greco-Roman culture that transformed Europe into Christendom. In the American experience, the life and work of John Lancaster Spalding (1840–1916) demonstrates an effective synthesis of faith and culture in the American context. As founder of the Catholic University of America, he provides an excellent example of infusing the gospel into the cultural domains of academia and education.

The Loaves and Fishes model emphasizes the evangelizing power of Christian charity. Jesus healing and feeding the multitudes is the Gospel paradigm of this model (Mt 15:29–38). Experience shows that the corporal and spiritual works of mercy performed by Christians in the name of Christ are evangelizing actions that have great impact. They not only communicate the love of Jesus to needy people, but also inspire others to turn to the Lord of mercy and compassion. The story of Rose Hawthorne Lathrop (1851–1926), the daughter of author Nathaniel Hawthorne, is one of the stellar moments of Christian compassion in American Church history.[2]

The conclusion includes some final comments on the proposed models, as well as the value and limitation of using models to describe pastoral activities. Before proceeding to the models, it is important to have a sound understanding of the definition, nature, and meaning of the apostolic work of the Church called evangelization.

## What Is Evangelization?

The first generation of Christians were indomitable evangelists. They were seized with the burning conviction that a great event had burst upon the world in the epiphany of the God-Man, Jesus Christ. "They knew that the world had been redeemed, and they could not keep to themselves tidings of such incomparable significance for the whole of the human race."[3] Certainly our Lord had handed down to his followers the missionary mandate: *Go, therefore, and make disciples of all nations, baptizing them in the name of the Father, and of the Son, and of the holy Spirit, teaching them to observe all that I have commanded you* (Mt 28:19–20). But it was not mere obedience to a verbal command that motivated the early Christians to announce the good news. They were interiorly compelled by a transforming encounter with God's own Son through the power of the Holy Spirit.

The first missionaries, which included both apostles and anonymous believers, were passionately devoted to the Galilean who rose from the dead. It was the hidden work of divine grace operating within these believers that transformed and emboldened them. They had been introduced to a new way of life and could not contain within themselves the discovery that Jesus, lifted up from the Earth, draws everyone to himself with his promise of eternal life.

This new and definitive covenant between God and humankind "was not made known to other generations as it has now been revealed to His holy apostles and prophets by the Holy Spirit."[4] Beginning first in Jerusalem, the apostles and their converts carried this message of redemption to the farthest corners of Earth so as "to open up for all men a free and sure path to full participation in the mystery of Christ (cf. Eph. 3:4–6)."[5] Their success was nothing short of miraculous. Within five hundred years, the Church had baptized and civilized the pagan world of the West, and taken into itself the best of Greek and Roman culture.[6]

Both yesterday and today this work of evangelization is the primary mission of the Church of Christ.[7] God wills that the Church evangelize, *"who wills everyone to be saved and to come to knowledge of the truth. For there is one God. There is also one mediator between God and the human race, Christ Jesus, himself human, who gave himself as ransom for all"* (1 Tim 2:4–6). Every person ought to be incorporated into Christ through baptism, in accord with the proclamation of the gospel, says Vatican II.[8] The same council reiterated the ancient Christian doctrine that anyone who knows that the Catholic Church is necessary for salvation but nevertheless refuses to enter it, or to remain in it, cannot be saved.[9]

These conciliar teachings summarize in modern concepts the same understanding that drove the first Christians to expend such courageous energies to lead others to embrace God's self-revelation. At the heart of this effort was a love for God and a desire to share with everyone the divine life offered by him through his Son. The work of evangelization gives great glory to God and realizes his plan for humanity, especially when men and women embrace the promise offered in Jesus Christ. As the process of evangelization advances, it anticipates the hope that the entire human race may someday become one family, one people of God, who, with fraternal accord, are able to raise their voices in unison and say, "Our Father who art in heaven, hallowed be Thy Name."[10]

So it is that in every epoch the Church goes forth to meet each new generation with the reconciling words of the gospel. The Church exists to fulfill this mission. As Paul VI exclaimed, "She exists in order to evangelize, that is to say, in order to preach and teach, to be a channel of the gift of grace, to reconcile sinners with God, and to perpetuate Christ's sacrifice in the Mass."[11]

The measure of success with which the Church carries out this mission has immense consequences in the lives of individuals and in history. The pages of world history demonstrate that the whole of human existence has been characterized by a harsh, obstinate battle for the hearts and minds of human beings. This struggle stretches from the very genesis of man and woman down to the present day.[12] Because evangelization is "the Church's effort to proclaim to everyone that God loves them, that he has given himself for them in Christ Jesus, and that he invites them to an unending life of happiness,"[13] it is the decisive factor in the outcome of this conflict as well as in the ultimate destiny of every person.

## The Need for Evangelization

Ten years ago veteran pollster George H. Gallup Jr. presented the results of his survey on teenage Americans. His findings were based upon the real experiences and perceptions of the youth themselves. The Gallup survey reported that the problems of young Americans are staggering. Violence, out-of-wedlock pregnancies, AIDS, drug and alcohol abuse, juvenile crime, and teen suicide are rampant across the nation among youth ages 13–17. Gallup found that many youngsters, both rich and poor, live in fear every day of their lives:

> In cities and suburbs alike, America's teens are meeting violence in their schools and in their homes…The twin threats of unwanted pregnancies and AIDS make teen sexuality more complicated—and more dangerous—than ever…Drug and alcohol abuse, pervasive among teens in this country, are linked not only with higher juvenile crime but with higher rates of teen suicide…Too many American teens lack the one weapon they need to confront the risks they face—solid values, rooted for many in religious faith.[14]

It seems hard to imagine that American children grow up scared in a nation that prides itself on its enlightenment, ingenuity, and immense resources. In the past decade since the report was published, these problems have only increased. If the general well-being of a country is directly related to the physical and emotional state of its children, then the United States is in a grave situation.[15]

The Gallup report concludes with a recommendation for healing the younger generation and consequently the nation. It calls for the inculcation of strong moral values into the lives of youth. It exhorts parents to involve their children in a community of worship; to set aside time for silence and reflection in the home; and to participate in religious services and not merely drop their children off at church or synagogue. Above all, the report recommends that children be encouraged "to put God first in their lives."[16] The fact that a secular organization like the George H. Gallup International Institute understands these responses as the solution to our country's problems is extraordinary.

Benedict XVI identifies moral and spiritual bankruptcy as the cause of society's ills as well. He says that the source of the unhappiness afflicting people today is a fanatical greed for pleasure and acquisition. This insatiable desire to consume and to indulge, he fears, has given rise to an anti-culture of death which is becoming the physiognomy of our times to an increasing degree. The unleashing of sexual desires, drugs, and the traffic in arms have become an unholy triad whose deadly net spans the continents ever more oppressively. Abortion, suicide, and collective violence are the concrete ways in which the syndicate of death operates; the immune deficiency AIDS has become a portrait of our culture's inner disease...The bodily immune deficiency is an outcry of the misused creature, the human person. It is an image in which the real disease is represented: the helplessness of souls in a spiritual climate that declares null and void the real values of human life, God, and the soul.[17]

Like George Gallup, the pope says that the cure of our postmodern ills must be religious and ethical: "Jesus Christ must be found in the present, and the meaning of the following words must be grasped anew: I am the way, the truth and the life."[18] Against this background, the mandate of evangelization takes on a new urgency. At stake, says John Paul II, "is none other than *the struggle for the world's soul*."[19]

While the fruits of the gospel can be recognized in the world in many ways, powerful, well-organized forces are also present that vigorously oppose the work of evangelization. The struggle for the soul of contemporary society reaches its zenith, said John Paul II, when these "anti-evangelization" forces seem strongest.[20] It is precisely here that the primordial conflict is being waged, and precisely here that people desperately need a personal encounter with Jesus Christ. Such an encounter will not only infuse new life into the hearts and minds of individuals, but it will also serve to redeem society.

## The Benefits of Evangelization

The state of affairs described above reiterates the fact that contemporary men and women are the subjects of a dramatic struggle between good and evil, between light and darkness. The origin of this discord resides within the person. Its source is an innate propensity toward evil that militates against the goodness inherent in human beings.[21] Within the core of every person there exists this tension, this duality crying out for resolution. At the same time there is a common recognition that this conflict cannot be overcome by one's own efforts and wisdom. While this tension manifests itself both individually and socially, the starting point for the resolution of this conflict is the individual person. As Fulton Sheen once remarked: "The tormented minds of today are not the effects of our tormented world; it is our upset minds that have upset the world."[22]

Reports like the Gallup survey illustrate that the personal and interpersonal tensions that plague humankind are not solved by human effort alone. The appropriation and expenditure of massive funds, the legislation of new laws, extensive psychological therapy programs, creative education initiatives, in-depth sociological studies, and the work of professional diplomacy have not resolved our personal and social problems. "This crisis today is so deep in its causes that all social and political attempts to deal with it are bound to be as ineffective as talcum powder in curing jaundice."[23] The cause of the conflict is the general breakdown of the moral order in human hearts. Because individual persons constitute society, only when they are regenerated and renewed can a collective restoration of society be achieved.

This is where evangelization offers the greatest possibility for hope, because "the purpose of evangelization is…precisely this interior change."[24] For when the Church evangelizes, she "seeks to convert, solely through the divine power of the message she proclaims, both the personal and collective consciences of people, the activities in which they engage, and the lives and concrete milieu which are theirs."[25] Evangelization invites all people to an entirely new life in Christ through baptism and repentance, which enables them to share in the very nature of God himself. When persons convert to Jesus, they are lifted to the supernatural order and "fall under a new government, their existence is ennobled, their life enriched, their nature elevated; this is the reward of their surrender" to Christ.[26] *So whoever is in Christ is a new creation* (2 Cor 5:17).

This regeneration of the person in Jesus Christ is supernatural; it has to do with realities that are beyond time and space. First and foremost, conversion offers "a transcendent and eschatological salvation, which indeed has its beginning in this life but which is fulfilled in eternity."[27] This is none other than the perennial gospel promise of the supreme happiness of heaven. At the same time, conversion to God pervades every aspect of human life by radically reorienting the whole person. It produces a definitive revision of values, behavior, and conduct.[28] Regeneration in Christ penetrates the soul,

> [it] roots out anger, resentments, and hate by overcoming sin;
> it gives the convert faith in other people, whom he now sees
> as potential sons of God; it improves his health by curing the
> ills that sprang from a disordered, unhappy, and restless mind;
> for trials and difficulties, it gives him the aid of Divine power;
> it brings him at all times a sense of harmony with the universe;
> it sublimates his passions.[29]

The convert also realizes that responsibility for one's neighbors and the building up of unity, peace, and justice in the community are personal obligations. In short, through conversion to Christ the human person is liberated from everything that oppresses, most especially from sin and the Prince of Darkness. It fills the convert with the joy of knowing God and of surrendering to the One who liberates forever.[30]

This reorientation has obvious social consequences. While the effects of conversion begin with the individual and relate to that person's ultimate destiny, they have temporal consequences of immense proportions. As the people who compose society change, so does society. Morally regenerated individuals act as a healing leaven within the community itself. "What we are asserting," says Christopher Dawson, "is simply that individual acts of spiritual decision ultimately bear social fruit."[31]

This is why it is imperative to proclaim Christ. There will always be fierce opposition to the gospel, but it remains the remedy for ailing humanity. Jesus Christ is not just the Savior of each person; he is the source of restoration for the whole of human race. He is not merely a great prophet or moral leader like the founders of other major religions, nor is he only the revelation of the Father to humankind. "He is [also] the restorer of the human race, the New Man, in whom humanity has a fresh beginning and man acquires a new nature."[32]

It is now easy to see the potential benefits of evangelization. It also is apparent why John Paul II said that "the starting point of such a program of evangelization is in fact the encounter with the Lord."[33] Conversion to Christ regenerates people, and transforms the temporal order according to divine principles. For both individuals and society at large, the benefits of evangelization are incalculable.

## Models of Evangelization

The use of theological models is one way of probing the issue of Christian evangelization. As Avery Cardinal Dulles notes, theological models are used to represent in an analogous way some mystery or spiritual reality "of which we cannot speak directly."[34] They are employed to deepen one's theoretical knowledge and appreciation of the reality they reflect. A given model must have a real functional correspondence with the object being studied if it is to be valid. It must "provide conceptual tools and vocabulary [to] hold together facts that would otherwise seem unrelated and…suggest consequences that may subsequently be verified" in practice.[35] Thus, a biblical model of evangelization serves to identify and synthesize a specific set of activities that we are inclined to believe about the process of announcing the gospel. Such a model can serve not only to integrate the empirical facts about evangelization, but it can also have an aesthetic value. That is to say, it can illuminate the mind but also touch the imagination and the heart as well.[36] It can stimulate missionary zeal and creativity.

Therefore, in developing these models, I present a conceptual framework that will deepen our understanding of evangelization and draw out its primary paradigms. I also reveal the beauty and spirituality that lie behind the work of evangelization. I hope that these perspectives will be inspiring and enlightening to everyone who is concerned with the paramount mission of the Church of Christ.

CHAPTER I

# THE ST. STEPHEN MODEL

Witness

*The St. Stephen model is based on Acts 7:54–60, which records the martyrdom of Stephen. It demonstrates the overwhelming power of Christian witness as a testimony to the gospel. All other forms of evangelization are effective to the degree that the evangelists are living icons of Christ.*

## The St. Stephen Model Defined

The story of St. Stephen is one of the most striking accounts in the history of the apostolic era. His witness to Christ before the Jewish authorities at the gates of Jerusalem has become a paradigm of Christian witness for every subsequent generation. St. Stephen, a Greek-speaking Jew of Jerusalem who converted to Christianity, was ordained to the diaconate by the apostles and commissioned to attend to the needy in the community. He was also gifted with charisms and *was working great wonders and signs among the people* (Acts 6:8). He frequently engaged the leaders of the synagogue in debate about the Messiahship of Christ, *but they could not withstand the wisdom and the spirit with which he spoke* (Acts 6:10).

Resentful of his apostolic success, his adversaries incited charges of blasphemy against him and had the deacon brought to trial before the Sanhedrin. False witnesses were secured to accuse him of blasphemy. The *martyria* (Greek for testimony) of St. Stephen begins here and ends eventually with his martyrdom.[1]

11

St. Stephen responded to the council in his own defense although he made no real effort to refute the charges brought against him. In a lengthy discourse he enunciated the Christian vision of salvation history in light of the paschal mystery. He concluded with a strongly worded criticism of their resistance to the Holy Spirit and their hardness of heart in not recognizing the fulfillment of the Mosaic promise in the person of Jesus Christ.[2] As St. John Chrysostom points out, St. Stephen "did not abuse them; all he did was remind them of the words of the Prophets."[3] He incisively presented "the position of Christianity vis-à-vis Judaism before the Jerusalem religious authorities."[4] By this Christian apology he knowingly courted death. In the end, St. Stephen's speech prompted tremendous fury:

> When they heard this, they were infuriated, and they ground their teeth at him. But he, filled with the holy Spirit, looked up intently to heaven and saw the glory of God and Jesus standing at the right hand of God, and he said, "Behold, I see the heavens opened and the Son of Man standing at the right hand of God." But they cried out in a loud voice, covered their ears, and rushed upon him together. They threw him out of the city, and began to stone him. The witnesses laid down their cloaks at the feet of a young man named Saul. As they were stoning Stephen, he called out, "Lord Jesus, receive my spirit." Then he fell to his knees and cried out in a loud voice, "Lord, do not hold this sin against them"; and when he said this, he fell asleep.
>
> (Acts 7:54–60)

Without giving him a formal trial, the Sanhedrin, which had no right to put anyone to death, lynched St. Stephen. As his persecutors assaulted him, he beseeched God to forgive those who both rejected Jesus as the Messiah and killed his prophet.[5] Bludgeoned to death under the impact of large stones, "Stephen the 'witness' [became] Stephen the 'martyr.'"[6]

The story of St. Stephen's heroic witness at the city gates "is concerned not only with the suffering of Stephen, but also with the spread of the Word of God."[7] It illustrates the two senses of the word *martyr*: the one who testifies to Christ by the example of his life, and the one who is called to make the supreme act of witness unto the shedding of his blood.[8] St.

Stephen leads the way in bearing testimony to the Savior. He does this not only in confessing his faith in Christ unto death, but also in bearing further witness to the power of Christ and his Spirit through immense meekness, patience, and mercy. By his virtuous conduct, St. Stephen proved himself to be "a genuine disciple of Jesus and imitated him perfectly."[9]

The essential point is that the New Testament account of St. Stephen presents an extraordinary paradigm of Christian witness: that method of evangelization whereby the believer boldly but humbly testifies by life and actions that Jesus is the Son of God, and that his teachings are the Word of God. This means of spreading the gospel does not usually require martyrdom, but in any of its various forms Christian witness is a powerful influence that disposes others to embrace Christ. Implicit in this witness is the virtue of courage in the face of resistance or hostility.

Behind every conversion to Christ one finds this witness. It was characteristic of the first Christians to a remarkable degree, and even inspired their enemies to convert. In the early martyrologies, we see that believers maintained a dignified and courageous attitude in the face of torture. They exercised charity toward their persecutors and patiently accepted their torments as the providential gateway to heaven.

This witness compelled observers and even executioners to accept Jesus. A great many others who saw and heard about these events would themselves later convert. The latent seeds of faith impressed upon their hearts by the noble behavior of believers would bloom into full-fledged profession in due time.[10] In fact, it was the witness of the early Christians that tamed the empire of Nero, Domitian, Trajan, and Marcus Aurelius. This wordless testimony, says John Henry Newman, caused "the proudest of earthly sovereignties" to yield "before a power which was founded on a mere sense of the unseen."[11] As the English cardinal notes:

> It is indeed difficult to enter into the feelings of irritation and fear, of contempt and amazement, which excited, whether in the town populace or in the magistrates, in the presence of conduct so novel, so unvarying, so absolutely beyond their comprehension. The very young and the very old, the child, the youth in the heyday of his passions, the sober man of middle age, maidens and mothers of families, boors and

slaves as well as philosophers and nobles, solitary confessors and companies of men and women,—all these were seen equally to defy the powers of darkness to do their worst.[12]

The singular example of these disciples conveyed a power that transcended words, or at the very least, gave credence to their words. The tangible demonstration of their adherence to Christ caused a crisis in the consciences of onlookers and opened them to the mystery of faith.

Beginning with St. Stephen, the entire history of Christianity reveals that the faith and fidelity personified in the lives of Christians is one of the most powerful forms of evangelization. After the Roman persecutions ended at the turn of the fourth century, the next wave of outstanding witnesses appeared. Many virgins and ascetics embarked upon the narrow path of prayer and fasting, first in their own homes, and then in the silence and solitude of the desert. St. Anthony of Egypt is the most famous of the "desert fathers." At age twenty, upon the death of his parents, he distributed all of his possessions to the poor, including an inheritance of two hundred acres of beautiful, fertile land. Then he withdrew to the banks of the lower Nile River to spend his entire life in prayer. Many men and women seized by his witness followed him to the desert.

The great witnesses of Christianity in the Middle Ages were often members of the monastic movement, whose lives of prayer, austerity, humility, and communal charity made them the spiritual champions of society. Led by the likes of St. Martin, St. Boniface, St. Augustine of Canterbury, and St. Bernard of Clairvaux, monks and nuns converted pagan kingdoms and renewed the spirituality of Europe by their witness.

The height of medieval Catholicism saw the proliferation of the mendicant orders, which drew people to Christ by their essential gospel living. The preeminent mendicant witness was St. Francis of Assisi. St. Francis often said to his followers, "We must always preach the gospel, and if necessary, use words." This expression encapsulates the St. Stephen model of evangelization.

After the Reformation, the Church experienced a spiritual rebirth that produced many saintly witnesses, some of whom are giants in the history of Christendom. One of these, St. Francis de Sales, hailed from Savoy. The mere sight of this man opened people's hearts to the Lord. His co-worker, St. Jane de Chantal, testified that "every Sunday and feast-day crowds of people used to come to him—men and women of high rank, ordinary citizens, soldiers, servant girls, peasants, beggars, people who were ill, full of sores, stinking of squalid diseases."[13] De Sales welcomed them all with the same love and kindness, making no distinctions as to class or appearance. St. Jane said of his witness to Christ, that, "unless you actually saw it, as we did, you could never have believed how very many there were whom he inspired with ardent longing to change their attitude to life, or to live more perfectly."[14]

A more contemporary example of the St. Stephen model of evangelization is found in the life of Blessed Charles de Foucauld (1858–1916). In 1886, this self-indulgent French military officer underwent a sudden and complete conversion, which prompted him to desire a life of intense prayer and asceticism. After spending six years as a Trappist monk, De Foucauld moved to Nazareth and resided there for three years. He was ordained a priest in 1901 and set off for the Sahara Desert, where he had once served in the French army.

In the African desert along the border between Morocco and Algeria he set up a hermitage in hopes of converting the Muslims who dwelled there. His mission plan was simply to live among the people he wished to lead to Christ.[15] Blessed Charles conducted a vocation of presence in which he "sought to bring Christianity to the Muslim desert tribes not by preaching but by good example,...contemplation and charity."[16] He had the heart of a missionary and, "ultimately, the method of evangelization he offered was none other than the one that had converted him...Love and make oneself loved."[17] This is the epitome of the St. Stephen model.

Blessed Charles was assassinated by a band of rebels in 1916. He left no disciples behind, yet his witness was to have a profound impact after his passing. More than forty congregations and movements have since been founded upon De Foucauld's spirituality of universal brotherhood and silent witness lived among unbelievers or the baptized who have fallen away.

In addition to those officially beatified and canonized by the Church, there are countless Catholics who have also typified the St. Stephen model of evangelization by living the Christian virtues in an extraordinary way amid the mundane circumstances of life.

In our world today, as in bygone eras, people put more trust in authentic witnesses than in preachers, or theories, or effective debating skills, or slick marketing techniques. It is holiness of life, the high standard of ordinary Christian living, or what John Paul II calls the "lived theology of the saints,"[18] that compels others to bend the knee to Jesus. Over and above preaching, "the witness of a Christian life is the first and irreplaceable form of mission."[19] The effectiveness of this method in disposing others to receive new life in Christ is verified by common experience, says Paul VI:

> Take a Christian or a handful of Christians who, in the midst of their own community, show their capacity for understanding and acceptance, their sharing of life and destiny with other people, their solidarity with the efforts of all for whatever is noble and good. Let us suppose that, in addition, they radiate in an altogether simple and unaffected way their faith in values that go beyond current values, and their hope in something that is not seen and that one would not dare to imagine. Through this wordless witness these Christians stir up irresistible questions in the hearts of those who see how they live: Why are they like this? Why do they live in this way? What or who is it that inspires them? Why are they in our midst? Such a witness is already a silent proclamation of the Good News and a very powerful and effective one. Here we have an initial act of evangelization.[20]

As every faithful Catholic knows it is the beauty of holiness "that convinces without the need for words [because it] is the living reflection of the face of Christ."[21] We call this way of proclaiming the gospel the St. Stephen model of evangelization because St. Stephen's dauntless testimony is the perennial paradigm of Christian witness.

## Example: The Jesuit Mission to the Native Americans

One of the most compelling examples of the St. Stephen model in recent Church history is the story of the French Jesuit mission to the

Native Americans from 1632 to 1672. Under indescribable hardships the Jesuit missionaries bore witness unto blood in their attempt to introduce the Native Americans to Christ. It is an example of Christian witness taken to a heroic climax in conformity to the Master, like that of St. Stephen.

The Jesuit plan of evangelization in North America called for the missionaries to set out alone or with one or two companions into the heart of the wilderness. There they lived among the Native Americans with the intention of evangelizing them one soul at a time. The Jesuits engaged the Native Americans in their own domains and learned their languages and religious customs. As they became fluent in the native tongues, they contrasted traditional beliefs with the gospel. As members of the tribes became disposed to the teachings of Christ, they were instructed and, after a suitable period of purification and enlightenment, baptized.[22]

After prolonged labor of this kind, the Jesuits were able to establish missions in Indian Territory. These missions were havens separate from but adjacent to ordinary tribal life. Here the Christian Native Americans could live a regular, disciplined routine, free of the native practices opposed to Christianity while maintaining many of their indigenous traditions.[23] In this arrangement the Jesuits respected their freedom and tribal culture.[24]

In the Northeast, as elsewhere in the New World, these missionary efforts were hampered by the activities of the secular colonists. The first French settlers in North America had their eye on the lucrative fur trade along the St. Lawrence River and in the Great Lakes region. With the intention of maximizing profit, they aligned themselves with the Huron, Montagnais, and Algonquin Indians. The fierce Iroquois were the historic enemy of these tribes and consequently became enemies of all the French.[25] These relations would have momentous consequences for the Jesuit missionaries.

Between 1632 and 1637, fifty-four Jesuits arrived in Canada to evangelize the native peoples. From there the missionaries ventured south into what is today the United States. They fanned out along the St. Lawrence and launched a mission that resulted in a blood-letting rivaling the martyrologies of the early Church. "The story of the sufferings of the Jesuits alone during the 1640's at the hands of the savages remains one of the most heroic tales in our colonial past," says John Tracy Ellis.[26] This mission began in 1632 and "ended in an orgy of fire and death as the Iroquois unleashed a genocidal war on the Hurons in 1648–49."[27]

The life of Fr. Isaac Jogues epitomizes this Jesuit witness to Christ. Jogues was born on January 10, 1607, in Orleans, France, and joined the Society of Jesus in 1624. He completed his lengthy Jesuit training without distinction. In 1636, just shy of his thirtieth birthday, he was sent to New France. Jogues was assigned to the Huron mission in present-day upstate New York. It was on the Hurons that the Jesuits concentrated most of their efforts in North America. The superior of this mission area was the great Jean de Brebeuf. Jogues and de Brebeuf both had premonitions of their ultimate fate.

From the outset Jogues was appalled by much of what he observed at this Huron village. Shameless immorality and pagan superstitions were commonplace:

> Each cabin contained a number of families. Only the dim light and the smoke afforded slight privacy, yet everybody could not but witness all that went on. That seems to have caused the Indians no distress, for the girls were allowed to be as promiscuous as they wished before marriage, and after they were married their husbands now and then lent them to a friend. But there was no consistent viewpoint. On occasion, when a husband became jealous—with or without cause—he might cut off his wife's nose or ears.[28]

Despite these conditions as well as the language barrier, converts were instructed and baptized. Jogues and his companions applied themselves to this work of evangelization, all the while realizing that the Hurons could at any moment rise up and murder them.

The greater danger was the fearsome Iroquois. The Iroquois federation included the Mohawk, Oneida, Onondaga, Cayuga, and Seneca tribes. They were the most cruel and treacherous Native Americans in North America. They were merciless toward their foes and exterminated every tribe that would not submit to their dominance. The Iroquois were at war with the Hurons and Algonquins, who were allied with the French. The growing influence of the French around the Great Lakes and the

St. Lawrence River infuriated the Iroquois and they were bent on the colonists' destruction.[29]

This was the state of affairs when, in 1642, Jogues was asked by his Jesuit superior at the mission to join a Huron canoe party bound for Quebec. The purpose was to obtain supplies for the mission and deliver correspondence. Jogues was free to decline, but he embraced the request without hesitation. He and two Jesuit lay missionaries, Rene Goupil and William Couture, joined the Huron convoy departing from the village. On the return voyage from Quebec, an Iroquois war party fell upon them in a surprise attack as they drew close to shore. In the onslaught the Iroquois captured twenty-two people and killed the other eighteen.

For sport, the Mohawks always tortured their captives. The prisoners were split into small groups and sent to various villages so that all the Mohawks could share in the delight of abusing them. The tortures included stripping the prisoners naked, clubbing them, gnawing their fingers and hands to a pulp, burning their flesh with lighted torches, tossing hot coals on their exposed bodies, pulling out their hair and beards by the roots, reopening their wounds, virtually any affliction that could be imagined. In the process Jogues had several fingers chewed off.

Eventually Goupil would have his skull split open for having baptized a baby, and Couture was enslaved in one of the nearby villages for a year. Jogues was held captive in another village. "He experienced several dreams while in captivity, one prefiguring his own death."[30] Jogues escaped through the help of the Dutch and returned to France on Christmas Day 1643.

The Jesuit missionary could not find peace in France. He longed to return to the Hurons. In the spring of 1644, he embarked for New France for the last time. Upon his arrival, he learned that he had been designated by the French government as their peace ambassador to the Iroquois.

The initial negotiation for peace between the Iroquois and the French proceeded favorably. Jogues returned to Quebec to give a report. In his haste, he left behind a chest containing some religious articles. At this time a deadly plague swept through the Mohawk country, wiping out many victims. The medicine men attributed the cause of the disease to Jogues's box. They threw it into the river, and developed a bitter hatred for him.

In the meantime, Jogues and the Jesuits in America decided to open a new mission to the Mohawk. Jogues and a young Jesuit lay missioner named John La Lande left for Mohawk territory on September 27, 1646. As they drew near to Camp Ossernenon, a band of Mohawks intercepted them and beat them. They were taken to the village to have their fate determined. The Mohawk chiefs were undecided on the matter, concerned as they were about French reprisals. One of the young braves took matters into his own hands. He invited Jogues to a feast and the priest accepted. As the Jesuit stooped to enter the cabin, he was suddenly struck from behind. The tomahawk blade split open his skull and killed him instantly. John La Lande suffered the same fate the next day as he searched for Jogues's body to bury it.

Hoping to build upon Jogues's witness, fellow Jesuit Simon LeMoyne made one of the last efforts to evangelize the Iroquois of the Onondaga tribe. In 1654, he went to live among them. Unfortunately, the mission was not successful and despite the best Jesuit efforts, it had to be disbanded in 1686. But a great light emerged from it: the Mohawk convert Kateri Tekakwitha. This daughter of a Native American chief would bear witness to Christ among her own and become known as the "Lily of the Mohawks," and eventually be beatified. Her "life and death became central icons of the Jesuit missiology in North America."[31]

Eventually, the Huron nation was wiped out and the Algonquins were reduced to a remnant. Subsequently the associated missions fell into desuetude. The constant warfare between the French and the English disrupted the missions and depleted resources that the French government formerly gave to the missions. The stream of French clergy who volunteered for New France dried up. The cession of Canada to England in 1763 and the suppression of the Jesuit order in 1773 were the death blows of the missions in North America at this point in history.[32]

Despite the demise of the missions, the Jesuit witness remains a poignant example of the St. Stephen model of evangelization, where authentic Christian witness compels others to consider the mystery of Christ.

## The Jesuit Missions Evaluated

When the French Jesuits first landed in North America and gazed upon its serene beauty, it was an unbroken forest save for the prairies and plains of the west and southwest. This vast wilderness was dotted with numerous isolated tribes of Native Americans. In dress, manners, and habits, these tribes appeared to be uniform. From the European perspective, language seemed to be the only distinguishing trait.[33] Despite appearances, the Native Americans were not a monolithic nation, but a vastly diverse people who were constantly at war with each other.

Some of the traits they did share were problematic for the Christian missionaries. While the Native Americans were not polytheistic and recognized one Supreme Being and Creator of all, they assigned to created objects supernatural spirits and sought to appease these spirits through incantations and magic. Their belief in the authority of ordinary dreams was also dangerous. In some tribes, if a brave was visited with a dream to do violence to someone, he believed that he was obligated to obey this omen in the waking hours.

Other characteristics shared by most Indian tribes were equally disordered. "In private life polygamy existed; woman was a slave of the husband; lust was unchecked even by the laws of nature and every excess prevailed."[34] One Jesuit reported that of all the moral precepts the missionaries attempted to impress upon the Native Americans, the one that forbade polygamy and marital infidelity was the most difficult to accept and obey.[35] Although "theft and violence were rare in the villages, in war every cruelty was wreaked on the captive, and every stranger was an enemy; war was an ordinary occupation, and scalps torn from prostrate foes the only mark of rank."[36] The Mohawks even paid tribute to their war god Agreskoue with ritualized torture and the blood of their captives.[37]

This was the field the first missionaries to America sought to conquer for the Lord. It was replete with risks and contradictions, but the Jesuits did not hesitate to engage this culture in the name of Christ.

Today the early European missionary is "regularly dismissed as one who showed no sensitivity to tribal tradition, who regularly violated tribal integrity, and who could barely discern a distinction between Christianity as a religion and Western civilization."[38] This allegation is debatable with regard to the sons of St. Ignatius. They were generally respectful of the indigenous Americans and adopted their way of life in hopes of converting them to Christ. It must be admitted that their understanding of the missionary mandate of Jesus and his gospel caused them to view with disgust many of the social mores and religious traditions of the Native Americans. The missionaries worked to eradicate these aberrations.[39] At the same time, the Jesuits distinguished between those indigenous behaviors that "clearly violated the essential spirit of Christianity," and cultural customs that did not, which they attempted to accommodate.[40]

Contemporary criticisms notwithstanding, the first Jesuit mission in America was a heroic but brief enterprise, lasting one century. The Jesuits could claim only hundreds of converts compared to the tens of thousands baptized by Spanish missionaries. Although the French missionaries had little to show for their efforts, "they left a permanent mark in the annals of American Catholic history."[41]

However one may view the methods of the French Jesuits, it is indisputable that they believed God alone was the founder of the Church in North America. They believed in particular "that martyrdom was the premier providential sign that God was directing the establishment of the Churches in the wilderness."[42] In 1639, Fr. Jerome Lalemant, SJ, a superior of the Huron Mission who narrowly eluded death himself, feared that the Jesuit missions in North America were floundering because no missionary had yet sacrificed his life for the cause.[43] Soon enough numerous Jesuits as well as Native American converts were martyred for their fidelity to Christ.

In the minds of those French Jesuits, "denying self, taking up the cross daily, and shedding one's blood as a witness to the Christian faith were the means of establishing God's glory in the missions."[44] Measured by external standards, that is, in numbers of converts, permanence and stability of mission foundations, and other tangible factors, the Jesuit effort to evangelize the North American Indian was a failure. "Measured by the missionaries' standards of Christian witness or by the criterion of human courage and dedication, the Indian missions were a major achievement."[45]

One must realize, too, that the fruits of Christian witness are not always instantaneous. In subsequent centuries, large numbers of Native Americans embraced Christianity, as they do today. Likewise, the Jesuit witness in North America has continued to inspire and direct souls to Christ for centuries.[46] Perhaps a portion of the Jesuits' missionary success can also be measured by its influence on later generations through the cult of the saints and places of devotion like the North American Martyrs' Shrine in Auriesville, New York. The recollection of their heroic embodiment of the St. Stephen model endures in American Catholicism to this day, enkindling a spirit of evangelization in all who hear of their martyrology on American soil.

## The St. Stephen Model Today

The Jesuit witness in the seventeenth century was characterized by its own historical context. The question is: How does one translate the St. Stephen model of evangelization into action in the twenty-first century? Over the succeeding four centuries since the Jesuits arrived, the mission field of America has been transformed. Once a vast expanse of desolate forests, lakes, mountains, and plains, it is now a populated, unified, socially complex, and technologically advanced superpower spanning from coast to coast. It is recognized as a Christian country, at least nominally, although this image is now tainted by visible strains of postmodern secularism and religious pluralism.

In the year 2000, Christians still comprised 80 percent of the U.S. population, but there have been significant shifts in the ethical-religious landscape of the nation in recent decades. Once rare phenomena, Buddhist temples, Hindu worship centers, and Muslim mosques are not uncommon today. New Americans, immigrants from around the world, adhering to Islamic, Hindu, Buddhist, Jain, Sikh, Zoroastrian, African, and Afro-Caribbean traditions, are now our neighbors.[47] Although a tiny minority, these non-Christian religious traditions create a new and visible dimension in American society.[48]

Over and above the religious diversity of individual Americans, there is a more dominant factor influencing the new shape of our ethical-religious profile. This ascendant factor is a pervasive secularism permeating the primary institutions of public life. For the past three or four decades, the legislature, the judiciary, the media, schools, and the worlds of entertainment and science have systematically excluded religion from the public square.[49] These powerful formulators of culture have filled the void they have created with intense and persistent doses of consumerism, utilitarianism, and the ethic of pleasure-seeking.

The challenge of evangelization does not end with the phenomenon of religious citizens of every kind immersed in a society whose laws and politics trivialize religious devotion and undermine morality.[50] In addition, the proliferation of sects and cults has also contributed to the spiritual paradox of the nation. The lure and impact of groups like Wiccans, New-Agers, Jonestown and Branch-Davidian sects, the Unification Church, and Scientology have made their presence felt in recent decades. Occult movements, witchcraft, and Satanism have also become overtly visible in our society. These groups operate with impunity under the current interpretation of the First Amendment of our national Constitution.

The number of Americans who profess no religion has also jumped from 5.6 percent to 8.8 percent in the past thirty years. Atheists have increased from 0.1 percent to 0.3 percent of the population during the same period. This last group has welded public influence far beyond their miniscule representation in the American population.

This panorama of varied religious belief, pervasive secularism, alternative cults, and outright unbelief exists in combination to produce the religious-cultural complexity of the United States in the twenty-first century. It "*constitutes one of the supreme missionary challenges of this, or any other age.*"[51]

In the face of this apostolic challenge, many think that the renewal of Christian life in the United States depends on overcoming the surface-level hostility toward Christianity by attempting to present the gospel through first-rate professional programs and innovative marketing methods.[52] Unfortunately, this will only bog down the Church in bureaucracy and internal agendas and deter it from making the proper response to the challenge of the times.[53]

What is called for is the St. Stephen model of evangelization, which in its very essence transcends all historical and cultural factors. In other words, the greatest need of the Church today is a phalanx of courageous witnesses who will endure *the time of great distress* (Rev 7:14) and whose *love for life* [will] *not deter them* (Rev 12:11) from giving fervent and prophetic testimony to Jesus Christ. "The Christian faith demands the heroism of the martyrs in our time too…even when there is no persecution, there is a high price to pay for constantly living the Gospel."[54]

Every member of the Church must be convinced that the renewal of the affluent, secularized nations of the West like the United States will come about only through the witness of Christians willing to endure rejection and martyrdom for the sake of Jesus' name.[55] "It is therefore primarily by her conduct and by her life that the Church will evangelize the world, in other words, by her living witness of fidelity to the Lord Jesus—the witness of poverty and detachment, of freedom in the face of the powers of this world, in short, the witness of sanctity."[56] Just as the Jesuits immersed themselves in the Native American society and lived among them as virtuous Christians, inviting them to do the same, so must Christians do today. The indifferent secularists, the hard-core agnostics, even the New-Agers, the Muslims, and the Hindus, must be convinced of the truth of Christ, but not necessarily by words. They must be evangelized through the holiness witnessed in the lives of Christians they encounter every day in American neighborhoods, schools, workplaces, and soccer fields.

Sometimes this fidelity is costly, as was the conversion of the Mohawk by the Blackrobes. St. Paul's exhortation is as appropriate today as when he first uttered it, *bear your share of hardship for the gospel with the strength that comes from God* (2 Tim 1:8). In this arduous task, the Lord assures us that we will receive *power from on high* (Lk 24:49) to carry out the mandate he gave us. As the first Jesuit missions illustrated, the success of evangelization "is based not on human abilities, but on the power of the risen Lord"[57] acting through the responsive and courageous hearts of Christians.

## Considerations for Christian Education

The St. Stephen model of evangelization brings to the foreground several important teachings that must be part of any religious education program in today's Church. First, the St. Stephen model emphasizes the importance of making the universal call to holiness one of the cornerstones of Catholic education. "All Christians in any state or walk of life are called to the fullness of Christian life and to the perfection of love."[58] This entails training in the Christian life of prayer, meditation, spirituality, the sacraments, the virtues, the corporal and spiritual works of mercy, and the example of the saints who have already achieved this holiness.

Although we have highlighted the heroic nature of the Jesuit witness in North America, the "ideal of perfection must not be understood as if it involved some kind of extraordinary existence, possible to only a 'few uncommon heroes' of holiness."[59] Catholic teaching proposes that a profound life of faith, hope, and charity is within reach of every baptized person through the grace of Christ. Each pursues this way of devotion according to his or her unique vocation and profession.[60]

The second consideration for religious education is the concept that each believer "has the obligation of spreading the faith to the best of his ability."[61] Implicit in the universal call to holiness is the universal call to evangelize. The context of religious education is the proper forum to teach every baptized person he or she has the duty to fulfill our Lord's missionary mandate. Were this to happen, Christians would "become powerful heralds of the faith. [This] proclamation of Christ by…the *testimony of life,* acquires a specific property and peculiar efficacy because it is accomplished in the ordinary circumstances of the world."[62] Integrating this precept into the hearts and minds of Catholics will be challenging.

Finally, religious educators should introduce their students to our Lord's own teachings on evangelization, the most extensive of which is recounted in Matthew 10:1–42. In this passage Jesus predicted that this personal witness of life will be demanding. He warned his disciples that in imitation of their Master they would be entering the mission field defenseless and vulnerable, *like sheep in the midst of wolves* (v. 16). He foretold the fierce resistance and persecution that his followers would encounter for witnessing to him: *You will be hated by all because of my name* (v. 22). He prophesied the clash of loyalties, even family loyalties, which the gospel would precipitate because *no disciple is above his teacher* (v. 24). Christians can expect to be rejected as Jesus was rejected.

In the face of this persecution, *do not be afraid of them* (v. 26), said the Lord; *What I say to you in the darkness, speak in the light; what you hear whispered, proclaim on the housetops* (v. 27). Christ exhorted his followers not to be afraid because he himself would empower them with the strength to stand fast, for *you will be given at that moment what you are to say* through the grace of the Holy Spirit (vv. 19–20). Jesus calls every believer to perfect trust and abandonment, and he says that persecution for witnessing to him is a great good; *it is enough for the disciple that he become like his teacher* (v. 25). Our Lord summarized the spirituality of Christian witness in this tenth chapter of the book of Matthew, and every believer should be taught to meditate frequently upon this text.

Jesus is also quoted in this passage as saying that *whoever receives you receives me* (v. 40). This statement is encouraging, but it is also weighted with responsibility. The potential for disrupting the mission of Christ is inherent in the call to witness. If the sins, failings, or broken trust of a Christian harm or scandalize those who do not yet believe, *it would be better for him if a great millstone were put around his neck and he were thrown into the sea* (Mk 9:42). Such actions constitute a counter-witness and can do more to undermine the spread of the gospel than virulent atheists or hostile cultures, especially if those at fault are leaders.

Conversely, the St. Stephen model of evangelization reminds us that, like the Romans and the Hurons, "the men and women of our own day—often perhaps unconsciously—ask believers not only to 'speak' of Christ, but in a certain sense to 'show' him to them."[63]

CHAPTER II

# THE JERUSALEM MODEL

## Liturgy

*The Jerusalem model reveals the power of the Church's liturgical life, especially the Eucharist, to bring people to Christ. Acts 2:42, 46a, 47 relates how the early Christians gathered together and celebrated the Eucharist. This sacramental worship has always been mission oriented, and by its very nature has attracted others to Jesus.*

## The Jerusalem Model Defined

The infant Church lived under the shadow of persecution, but it was undeterred in its fidelity to the "new way" of life offered by Jesus. The Jerusalem Christians continued to devote

> *themselves to the teaching of the apostles and to the communal life, to the breaking of the bread and to the prayers. Every day they devoted themselves to meeting together in the temple area and to breaking bread in their homes ... praising God and enjoying favor with all the people. And every day the Lord added to their number those who were being saved.*                               (Acts 2:42, 46a, 47)

At the center of this early Christian life was "the breaking of the bread." For the first believers this expression referred to a specific religious act: the ritual celebration of the Eucharistic mystery.[1] Each Sunday they gathered in each other's homes for the "New Passover" meal instituted by

28

Jesus. During this celebration of thanksgiving, they proclaimed readings, sang hymns, and offered prayers to God through Christ. After the president of the assembly blessed the bread and wine, the baptized consumed these elements, which they held to be the body and blood of Christ.[2]

The early Christians believed this celebration to be a sacramental encounter with the crucified and risen Christ who was made present through the rite.[3] This ritual, established by Jesus at the Last Supper, bore the character of eschatological fulfillment. It was a movement in faith toward the Lord that anticipated his promised return in which the liberation and unity of all created things will be realized.[4] The sense that the liturgy was destined to draw all of the nations into a universal communion of worship offered to the one God was an important theme in the mind of the primitive Church: *my house shall be called a house of prayer for all peoples,* says the Gospel of St. Mark (11:17).

The other sacraments and associated rituals completed the liturgical life of the early believers. During the subsequent waves of Roman persecutions, they thrived, and even increased in numbers, by adhering to Jesus through this sacramental life of prayer and worship.

At this point in time the Christian liturgy was necessarily simple and often secret. "As the Church emerged from the twilight, its public worship increased in splendour and impressiveness; but this was only the outward expression of a marvelous development of liturgical sense and understanding."[5] As Odo Casel notes, "The liturgy bore within itself so much of the seed of beauty that it was of itself bound to flower ultimately. But the internal principle which controlled the form of that flowering was the essence of Christianity."[6]

After the Peace of Constantine, the maturing sacramental life of the Church continued to be the centerpiece of devotion and unity for believers. As Christianity expanded throughout the empire and reached even to the frontier, the liturgy was not only the source of Christian sustenance but it also became more and more an instrument of evangelization. The Church's public worship emerged as the essential "means by which the mind of the gentiles and the barbarians was attuned to a new view of life and a new concept of history."[7] The liturgy presented in visible signs and symbols what the Creator had done and was doing for the human race. It majestically disclosed the history of redemption and the fulfillment of God's covenant with his creatures through the prayers and sacred actions of the paschal celebrations.[8]

The Church's sacramental life became a primary medium for impressing upon people and society the gifts and virtues of Christ. The secondary aspects of the liturgy such as art, architecture, music, and poetry also communicated the gospel message to believers and unbelievers alike.

Christian liturgy expressed spiritual realities with much greater intensity and with more depth of personal feeling than pagan rituals and devotions had ever attained, and at the same time it represented the universal voice of Christ and his Church.[9] As the liturgy developed to meet the needs of the times, it penetrated the lives of the people at many levels. It influenced institutions, literature, customs, and personal behavior:

> Take for example the case of the transformation of the barbarian king or war leader by the sacramental rite of consecration as practiced throughout Europe in the Middle Ages. This obviously did not convert the ordinary feudal monarch into a St. Louis or a King Alfred, but it did establish an ideal norm by which rulers were judged and which moralized the institution itself. And the same is true of the institution of knighthood, and still more true of essentially Christian institutions, like priesthood and episcopacy and monasticism. A Christian civilization is certainly not a perfect civilization, but it is a civilization that accepts the Christian way of life as normal and frames its institutions as the organs of a Christian order.[10]

Thus the liturgy served as the principal means of converting the disintegrating Roman Empire and its invaders into a new society called Christendom. In every subsequent age of history and in every corner of the planet the liturgy has proven to be at the heart of transforming peoples and nations into followers of Christ. This is why the magisterium of the Church takes care to remind us "that the liturgy is intimately linked to the Church's mission to evangelize."[11]

Whenever the Church is offering the sacred liturgy, it is engaged in the work of evangelization. It is not so much that worship is consciously being used as a tool for this purpose. The primary purpose of the liturgy is always the glorification of God. At the same time, when the community of believers is gathered together in sincere worship of God, the liturgy has a divine luminosity that becomes a call and a hope for those who do not yet believe.[12]

As the mystery of Christ is made present in and through the public prayer of the Church, it draws others into an encounter with the Lord himself. Each member of the assembly is absorbed into the sacramental contemplation of Christ and "swept along by that power straining upward to the Hereafter that runs through the entire liturgy," wrote Romano Guardini.[13]

The very nature and style of Christian worship promotes communion with Christ and openness to his divine truth. His Word permeates every aspect of liturgical worship. The liturgy "condenses into prayer the entire body of religious truth. Indeed, it is nothing else but truth expressed in terms of prayer."[14] In this sense it "is a model for evangelical proclamation."[15]

While the liturgy proclaims the Word of God directly, it also transcends doctrinal discourse because it is able to reach people on the aesthetic and experiential levels as well. It communicates the content and sentiments of the gospel to the whole person, appealing to both internal and external faculties. "In short, the liturgy is an extraordinary means of evangelizing man, with all his qualities of mind and the sharpness of his senses, with his capacity for insight and his artistic or musical sensitivity, which better expresses his desire for the absolute than any speech could."[16]

St. Augustine himself discovered this truth when he was meandering about the Christian churches of Milan in the tender stages of his conversion. Upon entering these churches, St. Augustine encountered choirs singing sacred hymns composed by his spiritual father, St. Ambrose. He recalls the effect the liturgy had upon him: "How greatly did I weep in Thy hymns and canticles, deeply moved by the voices of Thy sweetly-speaking Church! The voices flowed into mine ears, and the truth was poured forth into my heart, whence the agitation of my piety overflowed, and my tears ran over, and blessed was I therein."[17]

A century and a half later, another Latin father of the church, St. Gregory the Great, expressed the same insight:

31

If…the singing of the psalmody rings out from the innermost reaches of the heart, the omnipotent Lord finds a way through this singing into the heart that he might pour the mysteries of prophecy or the grace of remorse into this attentively listening organ…Hence in the song of praise we gain access to where Jesus can reveal himself, for if remorse is poured out through the singing of psalms, then a way to the heart emerges in us at the end of which we reach Jesus.[18]

The enduring testimony of the Church affirms that from the liturgy, especially the Eucharist, divine grace is poured out upon men and women as from a fountain, effecting their conversion and sanctification.[19] The liturgy contains this power because Christ himself, the source of every missionary impulse, acts in and through the Church's public prayer. The grandeur of the sacramental life reaches the hearts of those who are estranged from God. It also fosters the deeper conversion of the baptized and charges them with the duty to express in their lives and manifest to others the love and mercy of Christ.[20]

The liturgy then, is *the source* of Christian evangelization and in every respect nourishes, renews, and renders effective the Church's missionary activity. At the same time it is also *the goal* of evangelization, because it brings about people's initiation into and communion with Christ, making them sons and daughters of God by faith, baptism, and participation in the Lord's Supper.[21] The liturgy is the principal means of dispensing supernatural life to beginners and mature Christians alike. As Paul VI said, the divine life that our Lord offers to humanity "finds its living expression in the seven sacraments."[22]

Because "liturgy is the encounter with the beautiful itself, with eternal love,"[23] it is and always will be an outstanding means of Christian evange-lization. For our purposes we call this means of evangelization the Jerusalem model.

## Example: The Franciscan Missions of California

A prime example of the Jerusalem model of evangelization can be seen in the Spanish mission to the Native Americans of California from

1769 to 1853. At the center of this effort was one of the greatest missionaries in American history, a Franciscan priest named Junipero Serra. Born in 1713 in Majorca, Spain, Serra entered the Franciscan order as a young boy and was ordained a priest at age twenty-four. He earned a doctorate in theology and then taught philosophy at the University of Majorca. In 1749, at the age of thirty-six, he volunteered for the missions in Mexico and arrived at Vera Cruz at the end of the same year. This Spaniard would eventually become the *presidente* of the California missions.

Before we see how Blessed Junipero Serra and his fellow Franciscans utilized the liturgy to evangelize, it is necessary to present a sketch of the Spanish missions on the West Coast. In the sixteenth century, Spain was undergoing a great religious revival. Spanish saints and spiritual movements were revitalizing the Church throughout Europe. St. Teresa of Avila and St. John of the Cross reformed their religious orders and infused new life into Spanish Catholicism with their writings. In 1534, St. Ignatius of Loyola founded the Jesuits, a zealous new missionary order destined to preach in America. Vocations abounded, charitable apostolates multiplied, and new institutions of learning flourished. This "tidal wave of religious enthusiasm" would eventually "spill over into the farthest corners of the empire, in places like Santa Fe, Santa Barbara and San Francisco."[24]

Between the early 1520s and the founding of the last mission in Northern California in 1823, hundreds of Spanish missionaries crossed the ocean and labored to convert the indigenous Americans in the southern and western regions of what was to become the United States.[25] At first they spread out across the frontier to preach to the Native Americans, making daring treks into terra incognita. These early apostolic campaigns into the wilderness turned out to be ineffective and deadly. Nearly all of the initial engagements between the Native Americans and the Spanish missionaries resulted in martyrdom.

This state of affairs compelled the Spanish missionaries to reexamine their methodology. They had learned the futility of marching solo or in small bands into unchartered territory and realized that a new approach was required. The previous "years of experience had demonstrated the need for reducing the Indians from a dispersed, sometimes nomadic existence into a more disciplined, settled way of life. Only in this manner could they successfully be converted and civilized."[26] This effort gave rise to the so-called reduction mission system that prevailed in the West and Southwest.

In this approach a walled village was erected, and two or three missionaries and some convert Native Americans took up residence in the mission. Once a Native American was baptized and entered one of these missions, he came under the authority of the Franciscans. The mission settlement itself was elaborate. In many respects, it functioned like the monasteries of early medieval times, creating a large, independent economic and religious complex administrated by priests and brothers. It also provided a safe haven for nearby residents in the midst of the dangers or the inadequacies of the surrounding region.[27] It was the task of the converted Native Americans to draw in other natives from the area.[28]

The architect of this mission system in California was Junipero Serra. During the fifteen years Serra spent in California, he expended himself as the *padre presidente* of the missions that lined the West Coast. He founded San Diego (1769), San Carlos Borromeo (1770), San Antonio de Padua (1771), San Gabriel (1771), San Luis Obispo (1772), San Franciso de Asis (Mission Dolores) (1776), San Juan Capistrano (1776), Santa Clara (1777), and San Buenaventura (1782). His efforts also made possible the last twelve in the chain that were established by his successors.

At their peak these missions were very prosperous. For example, the twenty-one missions in California witnessed thirty thousand Native Americans engaged in farming, animal husbandry, and other skills taught to them by the friars.[29] A field report from Serra recounts a typical day at a Spanish mission:

> They pray twice daily with the priest in the church. More than one hundred twenty of them confess in Spanish and many who have died used to do it as well. The others confess as best they can. They work at all kinds of mission labor, such as farm hands, herdsmen, cowboys, shepherds, milkers, diggers, gardeners, carpenters, farmers, irrigators, reapers, blacksmiths, sacristans, and they do everything else that comes along for their corporal and spiritual welfare.[30]

At the heart of every mission, just like any monastery in Europe, was the liturgical life of the priests and Christian Native Americans attached to it. The sacramental and ecclesial worship (the Jerusalem model) offered at the mission became the essential means of introducing the California natives to the mysteries of the Christian religion.

Early on, Serra and his brothers noticed that the liturgy had a particular appeal to the Native Americans' highly developed sense of sight and hearing. Consequently they made full use of it to reach their religious sensibilities and to communicate the gospel. For example, the friars taught both plain chant and polyphony to the new Christians. They also set Christian lyrics to familiar Native American tunes. "Indian musicians performed in orchestras and choirs, playing instruments such as bass fiddles, contrabassos, and drums made in mission workshops."[31] This enabled the Franciscans to celebrate the great feasts of the Church in ways that resonated with the Native American sense of aesthetics.[32]

On every possible occasion the liturgy was utilized as an instrument for Christianizing the people. "The whole year was fashioned by the Christian calendar, punctuated continually by ritual."[33] In Advent, the missionary community conducted *Las Posadas,* "The Inns," a celebration commemorating the journey of Mary and Joseph from Nazareth to Bethlehem for the census.[34] At Christmas, the friars taught young Native Americans to enact the nativity of Jesus.

On the Fridays of Lent, Serra carried a wooden cross from the mission church to a nearby hill. Along the way of the cross, another Franciscan explained to the Native Americans each of the fourteen stations of the Lord's passion. On Palm Sunday, everyone carried a palm branch and processed with songs and acclamations, recalling the gospel scene when Jesus entered into Jerusalem. On Holy Thursday, Serra washed the feet of twelve elderly Native Americans and consumed a meal with them before the congregation. Then he elucidated the mystery of the Mass, instituted by Jesus at the Last Supper. On Good Friday the friars reenacted Christ's descent from the cross and his entombment. They used a realistic, life-size image of Jesus with movable limbs that folded in place as the Lord's corpse was set in a casket. During the service, one of the priests explained the salvific meaning of Christ's passion and death to the Indians.

On the feast of Corpus Christi, the consecrated host was enthroned in a silver monstrance and taken in grand procession throughout the mission. Four beautifully decorated stations were set up along the way, and hymns and prayers were offered to Christ in both Spanish and the indigenous language of the people.[35] These services left indelible imprints upon the minds and hearts of the new Christians.

The mission churches themselves were constructed in a style that combined Old World Spanish baroque with the adobe materials and designs of the Native Americans, producing the colonial architecture reminiscent of the period.[36] The beauty of these structures and their interior ornamentation deeply impressed the Native Americans and helped to elevate their hearts and minds to the transcendent mystery of God.[37]

From experience, Serra was totally convinced of the power of Christian liturgy to touch the hearts of native Californians. He did everything in his power to make each liturgical celebration edifying to those in his care. "On the feast of any Mystery or feast of particular importance [he sang] the Mass and divine service…[He] conducted [it] with all conceivable solemnity in order to make a deep impression, even through the eyes, on our poor converted Indians."[38] This liturgical repertoire was indispensable in introducing the California natives to Christ and sustaining their nascent faith. The liturgy in and of itself drew them into the Christian way of life. It was the hinge of the Franciscan program of evangelization.

In July 1784, Serra returned to San Carlos Borromeo mission after one of his frequent pastoral visits to another mission. This time he knew his end was approaching. Yet even in his final hours, his liturgical devotion drew the Californians to the Lord. When word spread among the natives that he was failing, they jammed into the friary and overflowed into the courtyard:

> His Last Communion was given with unusual solemnity; there was incense and the singing of the *Tantum Ergo,* which Junipero intoned in a loud voice as though he were in full health. He was always anxious to make an impression on his convert natives through the ceremonies of the Church, and on this occasion he wanted to instruct them, too, through his example. He remained kneeling at the side of the altar in deep recollection,

and when he got up and slowly returned to his little room, the whole assembly accompanied him, and many of the people were crying because they knew that their Padre was going to leave them.[39]

He died a noble death the next day on August 28, 1784. As the mission bell rang out news of his passing, the Native Americans flocked to the mission. The demonstration of reverence and affection by both Spaniards and natives testified to "the heroic virtues which they had witnessed in him during life."[40]

In the end, the Spanish missions were not to survive. A discussion of the merits, defects, and ultimate fate of these missions is presented in the following section. For now it is sufficient to note that the liturgical life at the California missions was decisive in attracting and forming Native Americans in the Spirit of Christ. It was instrumental in transforming them into the Latino Christian people that we recognize today. The Jerusalem model of evangelization was perhaps the most significant factor in this process.

## The Franciscan Missions Evaluated

Contemporary authors have differing views regarding the first evangelization of America. Thomas Merton called the colonization and missions in the New World one of the great tragedies of Western Christendom. According to him and other critics, it entailed the almost complete destruction of the existing Native American cultures by the colonists. The civilization was abolished on the pretense of idolatrous worship. Native Americans were inferior by nature and therefore legitimately exploited and oppressed by the superior white man.[41]

Recent criticisms of the Franciscan missions to the Native Americans of the Southwest also emerged when the Church moved to beatify Junipero Serra in the 1980s. Activists, both Catholic and non-Catholic, accused Serra and his confreres of participating in and even leading the demise of Native American society in California in the eighteenth and nineteenth centuries. Many of Native American descent from California and around the country joined in the angry outcry. They published historical studies to support their case.[42] As a result of this controversy, Serra's beatification, originally planned for the papal visit to the West Coast in 1987, was postponed. After a thorough Vatican examination, John Paul II proceeded to beatify Serra at St. Peter's Basilica in Rome on September 25, 1988.

It was not surprising that many Spaniards who arrived in the New World would consider the Native American inferior. The primitive nature of tribal life in the wilderness was in poignant contrast to the excellence of sixteenth- and seventeenth-century European culture. For the Spanish, then, the problem of evangelization also became a problem of civilization. The Spanish priest Fermin Lasuen, who was head of the California missions at one time, concisely explained this position. He wrote in 1801: "the greatest problem of the missionary was...how to transform a savage race such as these into a society that is human, Christian, civil and industrious."[43]

Such thinking can devolve into attitudes that pave the way to abuse, which did in fact happen. Many conquistadors used the natives and their holdings according to their selfish whim, although the Church fiercely objected to this behavior. In 1573, Paul III made an intervention on behalf of the Native Americans, affirming their spiritual equality and the brotherhood of all peoples. In the papal bull *Sublimis Deus,* he said that it is the "enemy of the human race" who has inspired the idea that "the Indians of the West and the South, and other people of whom we have recent knowledge should be treated as dumb brutes created for our service."[44] He commanded that the Native Americans, in fact, all non-Christians "are by no means to be deprived of their liberty or the possession of their property, even though they be outside the faith of Jesus Christ; and that they may and should, freely and legitimately, enjoy their liberty and the possession of their property; nor should they be in any way enslaved."[45]

Missionaries like Eusebio Kino, Bartolome de Las Casas, Antonio de Montesinos, and many others attempted to enforce this decree. Spanish colonists continued to exploit the Native Americans and even organized slave raids against them.[46] This behavior was a major deterrent to the evangelization of the Native American.

Although the missionaries defended the Native Americans in the face of flagrant violations by European colonists, they too were tainted by the attitudes of their day. As noted earlier, in the Spanish reductions of the United States, Native Americans were free to refuse baptism, but once they decided to be baptized they came under the complete authority of the Franciscans. The converts were not free to leave the mission without permission and those who misbehaved were disciplined. On occasion corporal punishment was employed.[47] Not all of the neophytes would take kindly to the rules and reprimands of the Franciscans. For example, trouble erupted at Mission San Diego in 1775, when two Christian Native Americans were punished for theft. They fled the mission, rallied the surrounding pagan villages, and returned to burn the mission to the ground and kill the Spaniards living there.[48]

Even though the friars maintained tight control of the reductions, it was always their plan eventually to turn the governance of the missions over to the Native Americans themselves. A diocesan priest would then take over the parish church at the appropriate time. When the process of evangelization and inculturation matured, the Franciscans wanted the Native Americans to be free to run their own lives.

Ultimately, the Spanish missions in America did not survive. The government of Mexico secularized the California missions in 1833. In the Franciscans' view this was done prematurely. The primary reason for this secularization was greed on the part of the royal officials. Epidemics such as tuberculosis and syphilis also caused the death of many Native Americans and decimated the missions. In 1848, tens of thousands of Americans converged on California in the rush for gold. By the middle of the nineteenth century, "the natives were either wiped out or driven off their ancestral territories,"[49] and the missions were no more.

For some, the controversy surrounding the California missions remains unresolved, but most historians contend that the defects of the California missions were primarily a reflection of the seventeenth-century European mindset. The supernatural motivation that drove this missionary effort is incontestable. The friars renounced home, comfort, and personal safety to follow the missionary ideal as the Church understood it at the time. Blessed Juniper Serra gives voice to these sentiments in a letter he wrote in 1780 to the Spanish governor of the region Filipe de Neve: "The good standing in which we [the padres] are universally regarded may be gathered from the consideration that when we came here, we did not find even a single Christian, that we have engendered them all in Christ, that we, every one of us, came here for the single purpose of doing them good and for their eternal salvation; and I feel sure that everyone knows that we love them."[50]

In our day, no one would deny that the first missionary methods employed in America had their shortcomings, nor would the Church propose the "reduction model" of evangelization as one to be emulated today. Vatican II has given us a more nuanced understanding of Christian mission and a greater appreciation of the inherent value of non-Christian religions.

Contemporary missiology would encourage missionaries of the twenty-first century to be Christ-bearers to unbelievers without political support or power, working in a spirit of humility, charity, and poverty.[51] They must always respect freedom of worship and conscience in their missionary endeavors. At the same time, the Church continues to hold that the initial announcement of the gospel must lead to individual conversions and baptism. Where they do not exist, the establishment of new ecclesial-sacramental communities is a priority.[52]

This "new evangelization" as it is called, cannot be new in content. The content of Christian mission is always the same, the one gospel given in Christ. As the gospel enters into new cultures, embracing their peculiarities and purifying them in the light of divine revelation, "it must remain the content of the Catholic faith just as exactly as the ecclesial magisterium has received it and transmits it," said Paul VI.[53] The pope reminded Catholic missionaries that with regard to non-Christian religions, "neither respect and esteem for these religions nor the complexity of the questions raised is an invitation to the Church to withhold from these non-Christians the proclamation of Jesus Christ."[54]

## The Jerusalem Model Today

Let us now leave aside the debate about the Franciscan reduction method in the New World and return to the main theme of this chapter, the evangelizing power of the sacred liturgy, which we have termed the Jerusalem model. As Benedict XVI recently noted, the work of evangelization "is the apostolic diffusion of love that is, as it were, concentrated in the Most Blessed Sacrament."[55] In the Eucharist, and in her entire liturgical life, the Church "announces the good tidings of salvation to those who do not yet believe, so that all men may know the one true God and

Jesus Christ whom He has sent and be converted from their ways, doing penance."[56]

The Church's liturgy, beautifully and reverently celebrated, leads people to behold the beautiful One and draws them to his heart. As spiritual theologian Thomas Dubay explains, "short are the steps from the experience of the splendid and the lovely to awesome appreciation, to a desire to praise, and, finally, to an immersion in prayer."[57] This is why Vatican II exhorts those responsible for the liturgy to extend themselves to cultivate liturgical beauty in the Christian community.[58] The transcendent reality of the Church's sacred worship not only requires the proper interior dispositions of faith, love, and humility, it also demands an exterior manifestation of grandeur and mystery.[59] The truth of the liturgy calls us to offer the Lord the best in music, architecture, art, planning, preparation, and all associated liturgical elements and ministries.

When it comes to the celebration of the Mass, "the Church has feared no extravagance, devoting the best of her resources to expressing her wonder and adoration before the unsurpassable gift of the Eucharist."[60] This applies to the whole of the Church's public prayer as well. The sacred liturgy, especially the Holy Eucharist, demands a setting worthy of the greatness of the mystery being celebrated; this setting is inimical to mediocrity.

The temptation to trivialize the divine intimacy offered to God's people in the sacred mysteries is counterproductive and counter-evangelical. The liturgical environment itself "must be capable of bearing the weight of mystery, awe, reverence, and wonder which the liturgical action expresses."[61] Care must be taken to ensure the liturgy is conducted with dignity, harmony, and grace, not only in liturgical appointments but also in movements, gestures, and actions.

By the grace of the Holy Spirit, the Church's rituals have the subtle power to enchant, persuade, and overcome the emotions and affections, and thus the entire person. This power, of course, comes from God, but to the degree that the Christian community offers the liturgy with beauty, reverence, and active participation according to the Church's norms, it disposes individuals to be touched by the Holy Spirit through the sacred rites.

In a sincere desire to honor God through worship that is beautiful, attractive, and evangelical, Christians must avoid the inclination to think that the supernatural efficacy of the liturgy is something they themselves contrive. Hans Urs von Balthasar tells us that the aesthetics of a given liturgy, although important, are not an end in themselves, they are not the essence of worship. Rather, liturgical beauty must fill people "with a sense of the holy [and] transmit a glimmer of divine glory."[62] The Swiss theologian warns that "the danger is greater that a liturgical community measures the success of a celebration by its own inspiration, by how they 'feel' or how they 'share,' rather than being simply open to God and His gifts. There are communities which—perhaps sub-consciously—celebrate themselves more than they celebrate God."[63] This may occur in traditional as well as in progressive approaches to worship.

The purpose of the liturgy is the praise and worship of the Triune God; he is the One who makes it efficacious. If a congregation has anything in mind other than adoration and self-oblation, wherein they mistakenly place themselves thematically at the center of the liturgy, then they are deceived.[64] "The community will celebrate merely its own happy pious feelings which were there already and which become strengthened through the meeting."[65] Everything that would distract the worshiper's attention from God and his presence, especially preoccupation with or promotion of self, frustrates the work of the Holy Spirit acting through the liturgy.

The key to authentic worship is the fervent, prayerful, and selfless participation of the faithful in the Church's ritual. "Like the passion of Christ itself, the [liturgy] has no effect except in those united to…Christ by faith and charity…To these things it brings a greater or less benefit in proportion to their devotion."[66]

In the post-conciliar age these points are crucial if the liturgy is to be a powerful means of evangelization.

The Jerusalem model also highlights another aspect of the evangelizing potency of liturgical prayer that has recently gained vital expression in the United States: eucharistic adoration. This practice of praying before the eucharistic species displayed in a monstrance on the altar extends the grace of the liturgical sacrifice[67] and, therefore, its evangelical effect. The work of the Little Brothers of the Sacred Heart illustrates this dimension of the missionary influence of prayer before the Blessed Sacrament. Founded on the spirit of Blessed Charles de Foucauld, this community of religious brothers is committed to a life of eucharistic devotion:

[They] live in mission countries, [and] there practice perpetual adoration of the Blessed Sacrament exposed…By taking the altar and its tabernacle into the midst of unbelieving peoples, they sanctify those peoples without speaking a word, as Jesus silently sanctified the world for thirty years at Nazareth…It is true that we do not take part in the glorifying of God, the work of our Lord, the saving of souls, by preaching the Gospel; but we do so effectively by taking to people the Eucharistic presence of Jesus, Jesus offered in the holy Sacrifice.[68]

From this sacred center the missionary heart of God radiates outward, drawing souls to himself. This means of evangelization is silent and unsensational, yet overflowing with missionary effectiveness.

Finally, the Jerusalem model reminds us in general of the primacy of prayer in the work of evangelization. Our Lord said, *I am the vine, you are the branches. Whoever remains in me and I in him will bear much fruit, because without me you can do nothing* (Jn 15:5). Because evangelization entails introducing men and women to the possibility of sharing in God's own life, evangelists are only channels who draw others to Jesus Christ, who is himself the source of this life. The work of evangelization is merely an overflow of the evangelist's own spiritual life. Without personal adherence to the one Mediator of all supernatural grace, the evangelist will bear no fruit despite Herculean activities and brilliant programs.

Divine life cannot be manufactured, but a disciple possessing a deep interior relationship with Jesus can become an effective instrument of grace for others. "We must build," says Fr. Malcolm Kennedy, "but unless the builders are united to God as the branch to the vine…unless Christ lives in them and they are transformed into Christ—the building is in vain."[69]

John Paul II made the same point at the turn of the millennium: "It is prayer which roots us in this truth. It constantly reminds us of the primacy of Christ and, in union with him, the primacy of the interior life and of holiness. When this principle is not respected, is it any wonder that pastoral plans come to nothing and leave us with a disheartening sense of frustration?"[70] Every evangelical undertaking is doomed to sterility if it is not fired by a profound spiritual life on the part of those who conduct it.

The Blessed Virgin Mary, sitting in the midst of the disciples gathered in the Upper Room on Pentecost, is the paragon of the Christian evangelist united to Jesus in prayer. She is the inspiration and intercessor of all who cooperate in the Church's mission of reconciling humankind with God.

## Considerations for Christian Education

In view of the liturgy's power to move the hearts of men and women toward Christ, it is crucial that the people of God receive sound liturgical catechesis. This education helps them "to open themselves to [the] spiritual understanding of the economy of salvation as the Church's liturgy reveals it and enables us to live it."[71] A key topic of this catechesis should be the importance of the prayerful and profound participation of the faithful in the sacred liturgy.[72] The celebration of the liturgy is not merely a clerical function performed on behalf of a passive congregation. In virtue of baptism every member of Christ's body has the right and obligation to enter fully into the Church's worship.[73] In order to do this the faithful need to know what the liturgy is and how to participate properly in the sacred mysteries.

If the assembly comes to think that the liturgy is a "festival of self-affirmation" or is driven by the "conceptions and practices of consumerism, entertainment and psychotherapy," then it is suffering from a false notion of the public prayer of the Church.[74] Catechesis today needs to emphasize the fact that God is the source of all divine life, and that this life flows outward to humankind through the rites of the Church.

In particular, the faithful should be reminded that the mystery of the Eucharist is a sacrifice that makes Christ present and offers him to believers in holy communion.[75] In other words, religious educators need to present and develop more rigorously three central themes in liturgical catechesis:

1. The Eucharist is a holy sacrifice that makes present in time and space the one sacrifice Christ offered on Calvary for our redemption.[76]

2. The body, blood, soul, and divinity of our Lord Jesus Christ become truly, really, and substantially present under the

appearance of bread and wine after the prayer of consecration at Mass.[77]

3. The main effect of receiving the Eucharist in holy communion at Mass is intimate union with Jesus Christ.[78]

If the faithful do not know what occurs before them and who it is they worship and receive at Mass they cannot properly participate in the sacrament.

Once Catholics have internalized these truths, they should be taught how to become deeply engaged in the Church's worship and how to enter into the inexhaustible mystery re-presented in the liturgy.[79] Full, conscious, and active participation in the sacred mysteries means that every member of the congregation has an important spiritual contribution to make in the liturgy.[80]

In this regard much has been achieved in terms of rubrics, liturgical ministries, and congregational singing and responses. Yet the interior dimension of liturgical participation has often been neglected. The faithful need guidance to help them realize that authentic liturgical participation occurs when, in the context of the Church's liturgy, believers offer the crucified Christ to the Father, and at the same time offer themselves together with Jesus in an act of personal abandonment.[81] The essence of this participation is an interior act of the mind, heart, and will. As John Paul II said,

> Active participation certainly means that in gesture, word, song and service all the members of the community take part in an act of worship which is anything but inert or passive. Yet active participation does not preclude the active passivity of silence, stillness and listening: Indeed, it demands it. Worshipers are not passive, for instance, when listening to the readings or the homily, or following the prayers of the celebrant and the chants and music of the liturgy. These are experiences of silence and stillness, but they are in their own way profoundly active.[82]

It will be difficult for the catechist to teach this interior art of liturgical participation in a culture that neither favors nor fosters meditative quiet.[83]

45

Likewise, it will be difficult to teach the virtue of reverence in a society that views respect for the sacred as something inconsistent with joy.

Despite the challenges, if these principles were at the core of sacramental education today, the renewal of the liturgy would be greatly advanced, and consequently its power to evangelize would also be enhanced.[84]

Lastly, Christian educators must explain to their students the evangelizing properties of eucharistic adoration, and exhort those under their instruction to offer missionary prayers and supplications before the Most Blessed Sacrament. As Christopher Dawson observed,

> the great cultural changes and the historic revolutions that decide the fate of nations or the character of an age are the cumulative result of a number of spiritual decisions—the faith and insight, or the refusal and blindness, of individuals. No one can put his finger on the ultimate spiritual act which tilts the balance and makes the external order of society assume a new form. In this sense we may...assert that the prayer of some unknown Christian or some unrecognized and unadmitted act of spiritual surrender may change the face of the world. [85]

The silent intercessions offered for the conversion of souls in the nation's adoration chapels may be more efficacious than thousands of sermons broadcast around the globe on satellite TV.

# CHAPTER III

# THE PROCLAMATION MODEL

## Preaching

*The Proclamation model of evangelization is the verbal announcement of the gospel. This proclamation of Christ's message also includes education in the faith that leads to Christian maturity. This is the mode of promoting the gospel that is most often viewed as evangelization. St. Peter's discourse after Pentecost (Acts 2:14–41) is the first recorded account of this method of evangelization in Church history.*

## The Proclamation Model Defined

The Proclamation model of evangelization calls to mind images of St. Martin of Tours traveling through the countryside preaching to the pagans of Gaul, or John Paul II explaining the meaning of Jesus Christ to a stadium full of young Muslims in Morocco, or Billy Graham making an altar call at a revival service. Proclamation is the most fundamental means of communicating the message of the gospel. It seeks to convert people to Christ through verbal persuasion so that they may receive him in faith and attain eternal salvation. All other forms of evangelization ultimately turn toward proclamation at some juncture.

Jesus of course is the greatest of preachers, and the spoken word was his primary means of announcing the kingdom during his public ministry. At his ascension he commanded his disciples to do likewise.

This command was heeded at Pentecost. The Spirit of God inflamed the hearts of Christ's disciples and drove them into the streets of Jerusalem, empowering them to proclaim Jesus Christ to citizens *from every nation under heaven* (Acts 2:5). "It was Peter, the one who had been living with the shame of having denied his Lord, who now emerged in his role as the rock on whom Christ would build his Church."[1] Assuming the primacy in this kerygmatic outbreak, he addressed the people of the city, delivering the first recorded sermon of the Christian Church[2] as he spoke for the community who stood by his side.[3] Raising his voice, St. Peter proclaimed,

> *"You who are Israelites, hear these words. Jesus the Nazorean was a man commended to you by God with mighty deeds, wonders, and signs, which God worked through him in your midst, as you yourselves know. This man, delivered up by the set plan and foreknowledge of God, you killed, using lawless men to crucify him. But God raised him up, releasing him from the throes of death, because it was impossible for him to be held by it...*
>
> *Therefore let the whole house of Israel know for certain that God has made him both Lord and Messiah, this Jesus whom you crucified."*
>
> *Now when they heard this, they were cut to the heart, and they asked Peter and the other apostles, "What are we to do, my brothers?" Peter (said) to them, "Repent and be baptized, every one of you, in the name of Jesus Christ for the forgiveness of your sins; and you will receive the gift of the holy Spirit..."*
>
> *He testified with many other arguments, and was exhorting them, "Save yourselves from this corrupt generation." Those who accepted his message were baptized, and about three thousand persons were added that day.*
>
> (Acts 2:22–24, 36–38, 40–41)

In this first declaration of the gospel, St. Peter summarized the apostolic proclamation that Jesus is Lord and Messiah.[4] He announced with Pentecostal fervor the good news of God's plan accomplished in his Son Jesus Christ: the paschal mystery of his death and resurrection, with all of its salvific implications. This message of hope was based on the Hebrew Scriptures and the revelation of Jesus. It proclaimed the great deeds of God in salvation history that culminated in Christ. St. Peter's speech exhorted those who listened to respond by living a new life in Christ, a life of holiness, contrition, and detachment.

St. Peter's discourse on the day of Pentecost was the prototype of the first sermons of the early Church and a paradigm of kerygmatic preaching. It announced the essential message of Christianity to those who had never heard it before. The kerygma possessed a new and startling authority that powerfully penetrated the hearts and minds of those who heard it. The inspiration that flowed from St. Peter's words, and the words of Christian preachers who would imitate this prototype, also supplied believers with the strength to endure the challenges that inevitably followed their conversion.[5]

From Pentecost on, the goal of all kerygmatic preaching has been the same: to introduce people into the mystery of God, who invites them to enter into a personal relationship with Christ.[6] As the proclamation paradigm shows, the specific content or vital core of this announcement is always "the person of Jesus Christ, that is, the preaching of His name, His teaching, His life, His promises and the kingdom which He has gained for us by His paschal mystery."[7] This core includes the entire corpus of Sacred Scripture and Sacred Tradition that the Lord entrusted to his apostles so that everything he revealed could be transmitted to all generations.

This apostolic patrimony is handed down to the human race in every age through the Church. According to Catholic faith, the teaching office of the Church is authorized to interpret authentically this sacred deposit of God's Word.[8] Genuine preaching, therefore, always conforms to the magisterium of the Church. This message, announced clearly and unequivocally, reaches people in the most fundamental ways, and awakens and transforms them into believing, practicing Christians.

This apostolic preaching is at the heart of all evangelization. By its very nature it possesses several distinctive attributes.[9] First, it is motivated by the Great Commission Christ gave to his followers to *go, therefore, and make disciples of all nations, baptizing them in the name of the Father, and of the Son, and of the holy Spirit, teaching them to observe all that I have commanded you. And behold, I am with you always, until the end of the age* (Mt 28:19–20). Obedience to the Lord is the impulse behind Christian preaching. A key aspect of this mandate is Christ's promise to be with the evangelist and also to impart his own authority to the duly commissioned preacher.

Second, Jesus gives his Spirit to empower the preacher sent forth by the Church. Preaching is a supernatural activity and the one who announces the Word of God cannot rely on his own abilities for success but only on the workings of God's grace. In this sense the proclamation of the gospel is not an event of the past. It is a living, ever-present communication of God's Spirit through the ministry of preaching.

Third, one comes to faith in Christ, and consequently to the threshold of salvation, through the preached and received Word of God. *And how can they believe in him of whom they have not heard? And how can they hear without someone to preach? And how can people preach unless they are sent?* (Rom 10:14–15). This proclamation of the gospel always has "Christian conversion as its aim: a complete and sincere adherence to Christ and His Gospel through faith,"[10] which leads to repentance and eternal life.

Fourth, an important aspect of proclamation involves the implantation of the particular church, the gathering of a community in Christ's name.[11] One effect of St. Peter's preaching on the day of Pentecost was the formation of the new converts into the first Christian communities.

In the task of proclamation, the preacher, infused by faith and aided by grace, communicates divine truth with boldness, fervor, and fidelity. Inspired preaching exceeds whatever public speaking skills the preacher may possess naturally. Without the infusion of supernatural assistance by God into the action of proclaiming the gospel, the preacher would merely be *a resounding gong or a clashing cymbal* (1 Cor 13:1). Similarly, the grace of the Holy Spirit assists those who hear the preaching of the gospel so that they may assent with the obedience of faith. The Spirit "moves the heart and converts it to God, who opens the eyes of the mind and makes it easy for all to accept and believe the truth."[12] The supernatural nature of Christian proclamation must always be appreciated by those engaged in the ministry of the Word.

Kerygmatic preaching was not the only aspect of proclaiming the gospel in the early Church. The Acts of the Apostles tells us that St. Peter and the apostles linked this first announcement with the more in-depth, systematic teaching called catechesis (Acts 2:42). The first evangelists were as much teachers as preachers, and the first converts were devoted to their teaching. This ongoing catechetical formation mentioned in Acts and developed over the centuries differs from kerygmatic preaching. It is intended to be a systematic, thorough, and complete elucidation of divine revelation. The initial embrace of the faith does not yield complete conversion and instantaneous knowledge of the mysteries of Christ and his commands.[13] A fuller understanding comes with ongoing catechetical instruction.

This broad and explicit proposal of the faith is indispensable if believers are to reach full stature in Christ. Without it, Christian belief and practice will remain superficial. Catechesis, therefore, must aim to form properly and completely those who already believe. It must lead them to an ever-deeper and more mature conversion of heart and mind, which culminates in a full embrace of Jesus and his way of life.[14] Catechesis also continually nourishes Christians as they strive to be faithful. The characteristics of this kind of education in the faith are:

1. It must be systematic, not improvised but programmed to reach a precise goal.

2. It must deal with essentials, without any claim to tackle all disputed questions or to transform itself into theological research or scientific exegesis.

3. It must nevertheless be sufficiently complete, not stopping short at the initial proclamation of the Christian mystery such as we have in the kerygma.

4. It must be an integral Christian initiation, open to all the other factors of Christian life.[15]

These features will ensure that catechesis achieves its aim of affecting a thoroughgoing conversion.

The ministry of preaching combined with catechesis is the most basic and perennial form of Christian evangelization. It constitutes the essential element of Jesus' missionary mandate: *Go into the whole world and proclaim the gospel to every creature* (Mk 16:15). The image of St. Peter preaching in the streets of Jerusalem is the New Testament paradigm of this form of evangelization, which we call the Proclamation model. Essentially it is a straightforward method of evangelization that has enjoyed success and widespread use since the day the risen Lord commissioned his apostles on the Mount of Olives.

## Example: Parish Missions in the United States

The Proclamation model of evangelization is epitomized in American Catholic history in the parish mission crusade, which reached its peak between 1830 and 1900. During this period, bands of Catholic priests from a variety of religious orders toured the country conducting missions at the parish level to enliven the faith of the people.[16] The preachers were primarily Jesuits, Redemptorists, and Paulists, although the Passionists, Vincentians, and Dominicans made their contribution to the mission movement as well. Most of the missionary priests from these religious orders working in the United States at the time were originally from Austria, Germany, and France.

In the nineteenth century, the period during which these missions flourished, the Catholic immigrant population of the United States grew rapidly. At the same time, Catholic life in most parts of the country was primitive; priests were scarce and funds were short. Many Catholics became inactive or joined Protestant denominations, which were more established, well staffed, and readily accessible. This was true not only of the frontier and the deep South, but also of the urban areas in the Northeast and Midwest, where tens of thousands of Catholics collected in ghettos and attempted to survive. In the cities, Catholics were deprived of religious support for the same reasons: too few parishes and too few priests.[17] The performance of religious duties consequently fell into decline, and apathy fatigued the immigrant Church.

As the Catholic population in America continued to swell, the bishops of the United States were aware that the problem was becoming desperate. They instituted a number of ecclesiastical measures to address the problem, but what was needed most was some kind of Catholic revival on the popular level.[18] The Church in America struck upon a solution and in the 1830s initiated the parish mission. This movement swept across the country, revitalizing the spiritual lives of millions of Catholics.

The parish mission was a phenomenon first developed in Europe during the Catholic Reformation by religious founders like St. Vincent de Paul (1580–1660) and St. Alphonsus Liguori (1696–1787). In 1625, St. Vincent established the Congregation of the Mission, known today as the Vincentian Fathers. This congregation conducted a perpetual mission in the parishes of the French countryside, working to increase conversions and religious fervor among the common people, parish by parish. From 1726 to 1752, St. Alphonsus preached and heard confessions in the peasant villages up and down the kingdom of Naples. Liguori's community, the Congregation of the Most Holy Redeemer, continued this work in his spirit and does so to this day.

This method of converting the masses was imported to America in the nineteenth century and was ideally suited to the conditions of Catholics at the time. The parish mission was a brief but intense dose of evangelization directed at the parochial level and designed to rekindle the faith of priestless, churchless Catholics.

In the first years of the mission movement in America, the preachers traveled alone or in pairs, crisscrossing the country by railroad, by steamboat, or on horseback. Life on the mission circuit was harsh. The fatigue induced by these excursions can hardly be appreciated today in view of the convenience and comfort of modern travel. Often the missionary had to reach his destination on foot through rugged forests and wilderness in every type of inclement weather.[19] The accommodations were no less spartan.

By the end of the century two to six priests constituted the mission band. These mission masters were on the road for at least six or seven months a year. When the mission priests arrived in a given place, people came great distances to attend the revival. They would spend the entire day in church, waiting to listen to the priests and go to confession.[20] If a church was not available, a barn or large house would suffice. Sometimes the priests had to preach in the open air and use a tree trunk or small embankment for a pulpit.[21] As Catholicism became the single largest denomination in the country, these missions gathered huge crowds together in both rural and urban settings. Even the turmoil of the Civil War did not deter the expansion of the parish mission movement in America.

A period of publicity always preceded a parish mission. The area was saturated with posters and handbills advertising the upcoming event. Local newspapers even posted the mission times, dates, and locations. The local parish priests visited the parishioners and encouraged them to attend. Prayers were offered for its success, the choir honed its repertoire, local men built a fifteen-foot wooden cross, and a supply of religious articles and books was made ready.

The mission was calculated to awaken people's consciences and jar them out of their religious complacency. Mission priests used stern, strong words and aroused great excitement and enthusiasm. They targeted their sermons to the emotions, and the effectiveness of the mission was measured by the number and intensity of the confessions.

The piety promoted in these missions was characteristic of the post-Reformation Catholicism that became normative in the nineteenth century. It was eminently personal, liturgical, and hierarchical. It centered around popular "devotions, the use of sacramentals, prayer before the Blessed Sacrament, novenas, and litanies concentrated on petitionary prayer and good works."[22] This spirituality emphasized "Marian devotion, the cult of the saints, veneration of relics, processions, pilgrimages, and other public manifestations of the faith."[23]

The mission itself was usually one to two weeks long, although sometimes it could go longer. During the mission, subgroups within the parish were invited for addresses intended specifically for them. Separate sessions were held for married women, single women, married men, and single men; sometimes children were addressed separately as well. Each day began at 5:00 a.m. with the celebration of Mass followed by a half hour of catechesis; later in the morning this cycle was repeated. The evening service began with a brief instruction followed by the Rosary. Then came the focal point of the day: the mission sermon, lasting a full hour. The evening service closed with benediction.

The instructions outside of the evening sermon were didactic. Usual topics included the sacraments of penance and the Eucharist, the Apostles' Creed, the Commandments and precepts of the Church, and the devotional life. Marriage and the other states of life were clarified. The intention of these catechetical sessions was to form and shape the religious awareness of the Catholics. The evening sermon, on the other hand, was a classic example of impassioned preaching. In the early part of the mission, it emphasized the horror of sin, the particular judgment of the soul, and the fear of hell. Toward the end of the revival it shifted to the topics of God's tender mercy and the virtue of hope.

The overall format of this series of sermons was common to all missions. It generally followed the themes of the four weeks laid out in St. Ignatius of Loyola's *Spiritual Exercises:* examination of conscience, the repugnance of sin, hell, the two standards, reforming one's life, the passion of Jesus, and the attainment of divine love. The preachers hammered away on topics such as intemperance, attendance at Sunday Mass, the duties of parents, and the importance of Catholic schools. The entire purpose of the sermon cycle was to arouse sorrow for sin, induce repentance, facilitate conversion, and rekindle fervent Catholic faith.

The last night was the climax and the cumulative effort of the mission usually produced the desired effect. One Massachusetts newspaper gave the following report of a parish mission in Newburyport in 1861:

> We are not unacquainted with revival meetings, and we have before seen people at camp meetings and other excited gatherings, stand up and vow; but we never before saw such a scene. The multitude looked as though they would have sunk into the earth or been burned together at the stake, before one of them would in the slightest manner have denied the faith. We saw before us both the material of which martyrs are made and the fiery zeal that would make them.
>
> During some parts of the service, especially at the farewell, the people were greatly moved. The speaker held them as by a sort of electrical influence, and the whole audience quivered like the leaves of a tree in the breeze. Now they sunk; and now the rising tide found vent in sobs and moans.[24]

Even if a particular mission did not have such dramatic results, it consistently reaped spiritual goods that perdured. [25]

At the turn of the twentieth century, as the Church became solidly founded in America, the centrality of the parish mission subsided, although it continues to be a standard feature of Catholic life. Today, pastors regularly invite preachers to conduct missions at their parishes, and the fruits of renewal still flourish through these visitations. This effort to convert others to Christ through preaching and teaching exemplifies the Proclamation model of evangelization.

## The Parish Mission Movement Evaluated

The first point that must be acknowledged in assessing the nineteenth-century parish mission movement is that it achieved the goals set for it by the American bishops. The parish mission inevitably left a wave of Catholic revival in its wake. There were innumerable sincere confessions, countless conversions, healing of parish schisms, great increases in parish confraternity memberships, and the widespread distribution of Catholic literature, especially James Cardinal Gibbons's *Faith of Our Fathers*.

The missions inspired a general invigoration of parish life, and even the conversion of some non-Catholics who were invited to attend the mission on the final day. "The revival did indeed foster a new religious experience for Catholic Americans."[26] It invigorated their spiritual life and instilled in them a strong identification with Catholicism. The parish mission provided a successful means of keeping Catholics in the fold despite the scarcity of priests and parishes. In all of its main features the parish mission proved to be the brief but intense dose of evangelization the bishops hoped would save the immigrant Church of the nineteenth century from dissipation.

In hindsight, there are certain aspects of the mission movement that are criticized today. For example, the preaching and general focus of the missions are faulted for being overly individualistic.[27] It is said that the emphasis was weighted too heavily in favor of personal salvation to the exclusion of social concerns. Connected to the theme of individual salvation was a tone of moral rigor and fear of damnation as the primary motivation for repentance. These features were present in parish missions, but it must be remembered that this mentality was characteristic of nineteenth-century Catholicism in general. The dominant orientation of immigrant Catholics of that period emphasized these qualities:

> moral rectitude, asceticism, opposition to the spirit of the world, and meditation on the great truths of death and hell to evoke a change of life. The religious experience that supported such an interpretation was typical of nineteenth-century piety...a strong sense of personal sin joined with a desire for perfection and a sense of God's presence; an exacting program

of self-discipline; a close dependence on Jesus, Mary, and the saints; and a reliance on the sacramental ministrations of the church.[28]

Moreover, rugged individualism was a universally recognized trait of an American citizen, Protestant or Catholic.[29] Even though the parish mission spirituality was individualistic, it was not devoid of a social dimension. The parish revival "was more than just a religious phenomenon. It was a social movement which strived for the collective conversion of American Catholics."[30] The missions succeeded in this objective. On the local level, pastors commented that after a mission the diverse members of their parishes became a united people. There was also a significant upswing in memberships in parish organizations of every kind.

Today, of course, the importance of the gospel mandate for social reform is appreciated, and preachers tend to avoid fire and brimstone sermons to evoke conversions. Yet, it is unreasonable to expect current theological concerns and developments to be the primary focal points of every age of Christian history.

Another aspect of nineteenth-century parish missions that is disparaged is emotionalism. It is true that emotional expressions were characteristic of many parish missions, but they were, in fact, joined to moments of real interior conversion. For ordinary Catholics of the time, the parish revival constituted "a special moment when God was present in their midst in an extraordinary manner."[31] The "people believed that the power of the divine was working in mysterious and surprising ways."[32] For the majority of Catholics, these emotional displays were signs of a great parish mission.

Related to the emotional aspects of the parish mission is the criticism that the preacher's approach was anti-intellectual. This was not necessarily true; the great missioners of the revival movement were the best educated men in the Catholic community. The mission itself included sound, systematic doctrinal instruction. We must recall that the venue of the parish mission was not Notre Dame Cathedral, where the renowned Jean Lacordaire preached to the cultured nineteenth-century Parisians. Parish missioners preached in the farms, fields, barns, and log chapels of the American frontier, as well as the ghettos of industrialized American cities. The situation called for straightforward candor, simplicity, and

concrete expressions aimed at reaching immigrant Catholics on the affec-
tive level.

Finally, some critics today denounce the parish mission as fostering an
ecclesial structure that was institutional, authoritarian, and clerical.[33] The
parish missions revolved around the preacher-priests and were animated by
the sacramental system of Catholicism. In the face of this criticism we must
recall the essential nature of Catholicism, which is sacramental. It is self-
evident from the success of the mission movement that the faithful rejoiced
to see the black-robed missioners trudge into their outlying district or
urban quarter after a grueling missionary excursion. They were Catholics
who for months, years, or even decades had been deprived of the consola-
tions of the Church's sacraments.

Today we certainly appreciate the importance of the laity and their
indispensable role in the mission of the Church, and we are the beneficiaries
of the ecclesiological insights and developments of Vatican II. At the same
time, we profess a sacramental faith based upon Holy Orders, which is the
essence of the apostolic faith. Catholics will always need their priests, and
this need is more acutely felt where priests are in short supply.

If we consider the parish mission in its historical context, it is without doubt one of the great moments of the Proclamation model of evangelization in American Catholicism. As missioner St. John Neumann says:
"He that has not given missions nor heard confessions during missions
cannot know how useful these exercises are. Owing to the manner in
which the Bread of the Divine Word is broken, when eternal truths are
methodically exposed to the hearers who have assembled in great numbers,
it is nearly impossible for them not to be converted."[34]

## The Proclamation Model Today

The demand for an effective Proclamation model in the life of the
Church today is as pressing as it was in the nineteenth century. As the
fathers of Vatican II said in the opening paragraph of the *Dogmatic
Constitution on the Church,* "Christ is the light of humanity; and it is, accord-
ingly, the heart-felt desire of this sacred council...that, by proclaiming His
Gospel to every creature, it may bring to all men the light of Christ."[35]

The centrality of the Christian proclamation has always been stressed by Church leaders. They remind us that despite the variety of means currently available to promote the gospel, at some point the witness of Christians must become verbal because the message of the gospel is not self-evident. Sooner or later there needs to be a clear and unequivocal announcement of divine revelation combined with sound, thorough catechesis.[36]

An American prelate recently highlighted the importance of the Proclamation model at the chrism Mass in his Boston cathedral. Addressing his priests in particular, Sean Cardinal O'Malley said that "today, with religious illiteracy at an all-time high, we must toil to preach and to teach...We must be convinced that the kingdom of God is spread by word of mouth."[37]

As Cardinal O'Malley explained to his priests, "the problem is that we are not convinced that preaching must be our priority," despite the fact that the pope, the council and our people tell us that this is the most important task of the priest.[38] Continuing in this vein, he cited a survey showing the direct relationship between the quality of preaching and attendance at Catholic churches:

> A national opinion research center conducted extensive surveys with the Catholic laity and was forced to conclude that the strongest correlation of church attendance and Catholic identification for both the young people and the general Catholic population were not issues of sex, birth control, abortion and the ordination of women; rather the strongest predictor of Catholic behavior and identification was the quality of the Sunday sermon preached in the respondent's parish church. In another survey of 30-year-olds returning to the church, the two most important factors were a personal relationship with the priest and the quality of preaching.[39]

This survey indicates that in America today, any program of evangelization has to include a plan to promote and upgrade the ministry of preaching if it is going to make a difference.

If only 22 percent of Catholics in America attend Mass on Sundays, the question arises, how does all of this emphasis on preaching help those most in need of evangelization, that is, the unchurched? As Cardinal O'Malley asks, "Are we preaching to the choir?" He answers, "Yes, definitely, but if we touch their hearts then the choir will become the messengers and the inviters…They will become evangelizers because we have given them the tools and the motivation."[40] Anointed preaching inflames the faith of believers and inspires them to become apostles in their own right.

At the same time, good preaching has an inherent power to convert the unchurched as well. The truth of this statement has been affirmed in a revealing study entitled *Surprising Insights from the Unchurched,* by Protestant author Thom S. Rainer, dean of the Billy Graham School of Missions, Evangelism and Church Growth.[41] Rainer and his team polled a group of 353 unchurched people who are now attending Christian services. All of these persons were at one time inactive in church life and now have become practicing evangelicals. To supplement this data, Rainer also interviewed 101 pastors of churches who have proven success with the unchurched. These samples came from referrals from two thousand active evangelical churches across the nation. Every major geographic region, as well as a cross section of all socioeconomic, ethnic, and racial groups are represented in this study.

The cumulative results of the poll showed that 90 percent of the unchurched were led to become active in a particular church *because of the quality of the pastor's preaching.*[42] The data overwhelmingly substantiated the fact that preaching was the most decisive factor in evangelizing the unchurched.

Rainer's interviews with the pastors of churches that have an effective ministry to the unchurched further demonstrated the importance of good preaching. The pastors were a diverse group: Anglos, African Americans, Hispanics, Asians, young and old, from the suburbs, cities, countryside, and small towns. These successful pastors were enthusiastic about the gospel and passionately desired to spread the Word of God. They rated integrity, personal example, vibrant prayer life, and intense Bible study as their leading characteristics.

The main point is that for these pastors who related well to the unchurched, good preaching was the priority of their pastoral ministry.[43] Rainer's findings suggest that preaching may be the most decisive factor in any curriculum of evangelization. Unfortunately, many programs designed to reach the unchurched do not even remotely take this factor into consideration.

An important corollary to the value of good preaching is the integrity of doctrine. Cardinal O'Malley explained that people are looking for certainty amid the cacophony of voices claiming to speak the truth today. He said that sound doctrine is an actual grace that the people of God need today. It enables them "to resist the temptation to conform to the culture of death, to consumerism, hedonism, individualism. The good news needs to be preached with clarity. No one will follow an uncertain trumpet blast."[44] Cardinal Dulles also asserts this point: "To evangelize, we must allow the testimony of God, of the apostles, and of the Church to speak through us. This we cannot do with confidence and success unless we have assured ourselves that the testimony is credible and unless we are able to convince others that this is the case."[45]

A recent study by Colleen Carroll, a twenty-seven-year-old journalist from St. Louis, also discovered the appeal of Christian authenticity. In her book *The New Faithful: Why Young Adults Are Embracing Christian Orthodoxy,* Carroll reports on a trend currently emerging among people in their twenties and thirties. Her research reveals that there is a movement within this age group to live an orthodox Christian life in an authentic, compelling way.[46]

Conducting interviews from coast to coast, among all denominations, Carroll documents a "small but growing core" of dedicated and committed young adults latent within many Christian communities who are educated, competent, healthy, and capable of religious leadership.[47] Their spiritual journey to orthodox Christianity began with "a desire too deep to be explained by sociology, too timeless to be particular to Generation X and its famous 'spiritual hunger.'"[48] Ultimately, the appeal of orthodoxy for these young people is the same as that observed by O'Malley. As Carroll testifies, "I have heard them speak of their weariness with secularism, their thirst for meaning, and their conviction that they will not repeat the mistakes of the generation that preceded them."[49]

Carroll's argument converges with the mind of Vatican II, which maintains that a successful curriculum of evangelization must be faithful to the apostolic tradition in both content and expression.[50] As St. Paul said in one of his pastoral instructions, people do not need interminable myths, idle speculation, or meaningless talk; rather, preachers should strive for *the plan of God that is to be received by faith. The aim of this instruction is love from a pure heart, a good conscience, and a sincere faith* (1 Tim 1:4–5).

With these various reflections on the Proclamation model in mind, I would like to recommend once again the parish mission. It continues to retain all of its efficacy as an excellent starting point for the re-evangelization of parochial life even today. As the number of priests in the United States declines, many regions of the country find themselves in a situation not unlike that of the nineteenth century. Priests are scarce, Catholic immigrants lack proper sacramental care, and parishes yearn for spiritual refreshment. Once again the parish mission can offer that injection of life and devotion that revivifies flagging or priestless parishes and reaches out to the unchurched.

Some of the same techniques should be recovered that made the earlier missions so successful. When a parish is hosting a mission, the locality should be saturated with fliers and posters announcing the event. Press releases to local newspapers and radio stations with the times, dates, and locations of the mission are an advantageous means of publicity. The parish choirs and organizations should also be drawn into the preparation and execution of the mission. The practice of targeting specific segments within the community such as single men or young mothers is also a feature that always attracts additional participants. Church members should be encouraged to invite their neighbors and friends, especially those who do not attend church, just as parishioners hosting a mission did 150 years ago.

It would also be good if the mission preachers themselves could arrive early and visit the taverns and markets beforehand. Mingling with the people on the streets and extending personal invitations to attend the mission was always an effective way of filling the house. Perhaps more important, these techniques can establish contacts with today's alienated and fallen-away members. In general, the creation of a sense of drama, excitement, and expectation prior to the mission is what drives its success.

It is still possible to find great preachers who are dedicated to this work. When administered properly, the parish mission provides a practical, straightforward, and readily available means of energizing the parish community. Fortunately, missions can be arranged with relative ease and at minimal cost virtually anywhere in the nation.   ·

## Considerations for Christian Education

Our analysis of the Proclamation model of evangelization highlights several issues for religious educators. First, the Catholic faith obliges the person who has been given the responsibility to preach or teach in the name of the Church to represent the truths of Christianity according to the received tradition of the Catholic Church. By preaching and teaching we mean the announcement of the gospel and the catechetical instruction given in the essential formation of Christians.

The ministry of preaching and teaching may be distinguished from theological research, which can entail speculative and experimental investigations. Even here there are limits to what may be taught, if it has the effect of undermining those doctrines that have been solemnly defined by the Church's magisterium, or have been taught by her ordinary universal teaching authority as binding on the consciences of all the faithful.[51]

Although there are different responses warranted by different levels of magisterial teaching, those who seek the message of Christ and his Church have a right to hear it without mutation or adulteration.[52] People cannot arrive at personal conversion without the light of God's truth.[53]

Second, the Proclamation model underlines the importance of homiletic training for priests and deacons. Because preaching is the primary way in which people are exposed to the gospel, this means that those who preach should be well formed and prepared for the task. Sound biblical and theological education has always been underscored in the formation of future priests and deacons. Today it is essential to give greater attention to the ministry of preaching, and to develop programs that enhance the methodology, preparation, and delivery of sermons. Also, there may be room for improvement in the preaching and communications skills of many rank-and-file parish priests.

Preachers may need to invest more time and effort in homily preparation. Rainer's study showed that more than 90 percent of Protestant pastors in America spend only two hours per week preparing Sunday sermons, yet those pastors who excel at reaching out to the unchurched spend twenty-two hours per week in homily preparation.[54] For obvious reasons, Catholic preachers also need to consider spending more time on this task and delegating other duties.

Third, religious educators today must appreciate the fact that "evangelization is an indispensable point of reference for catechesis."[55] Those who participate in the work of catechesis need to see themselves as evangelists, disciples of Christ who are called to invite those in their pastoral care to total conversion in Christ. "In a nutshell, we cannot presume as a given in our catechetical efforts even a foundational level of understanding and adhesion to the faith. Rather we must approach the task as if we were introducing our students and hearers to Christ for the first time."[56]

Even after the first conversion, evangelical catechesis is integral to each Christian's lifelong spiritual passage. Education in the faith is required at every level to accompany believers along the "ascent of Mount Carmel," St. John of the Cross's allegory for complete union with Christ. The demanding nature of the work is why Christian educators are among the most dedicated and self-sacrificing ministers in the Church.

Fourth, while preachers or teachers have to work as if everything depended on their efforts, they must recall that the ultimate efficacy of their ministry is essentially dependent upon supernatural factors. The art or science of communicating the Word of God has more to do with one's relationship with Christ and quest for virtue than it does with methodology and technique. In other words, the most effective pedagogy for any proclaimer of the gospel is the "pedagogy of holiness."[57] The great masters of communicating the Word of God tell us that the catechist and preacher will be able to touch souls with the good news of Jesus Christ to the degree that they are in union with him.[58]

Fifth, religious educators should encourage those in their charge to look for opportunities to propagate the gospel in the ordinary settings of life. Every Christian can offer others a personal word of kindness, consolation, or direction in a religious context at moments of trial and sickness as well as occasions of joy and thanksgiving. In the car, on the street, in offices, schools, and homes, easy, genial exchanges that draw near to the most important issues of life, death, God, and the soul provide the forums for gently communicating the gospel. This is never a question of winning a debate or engaging in polemics. Neither should there be a false shame or harsh self-assertiveness in one's tone. Rather, the believing Catholic attempts to share supernatural hope and joy with anyone who needs it or is looking for it.[59] Simply said, there are times when it is a sin to be silent.

Finally, ministers of the Word today must fully utilize the new means of preaching and teaching that modern technology supplies. Radio, television, film, music, the Internet, the print media, and other means of social communication have tremendous appeal and influence in the modern world. In fact, the media may be the most dominant influence upon our culture today. Vatican II urged all of the members of the Church to make use of these forms of communication to promote the gospel and its values.[60] In this area, Catholics also have much to learn from our evangelical brothers and sisters.

CHAPTER IV

# THE FRATERNITY MODEL

## Small Communities

*According to the Fraternity model, a core group of devoted, well-trained disciples is formed and sent forth to evangelize. This was the method the Lord himself used to spread the gospel to the ends of the Earth. Mark 3:13–19 recounts Jesus' calling, forming, empowering, and commissioning his apostles. This group of twelve constituted the evangelical nucleus that propagated the message of salvation throughout the entire Roman Empire and beyond. The Fraternity model highlights the importance of small, well-formed communities in carrying out the Church's mission of evangelization.*

## The Fraternity Model Defined

It was a decision of eternal importance that Jesus took to prayer that night: he had come to the point in his ministry where he had to choose his closest associates.[1] He ascended the mountain to deliberate upon the matter in dialogue with his Father. Jesus was now ready to set aside from among his many disciples a few who would be his most intimate and trusted collaborators,[2] those he would draw together to entrust the mission of extending his kingdom to the ends of the Earth until his final return.[3] On the mountain that night he prayerfully selected his inner circle and:

*summoned those whom he wanted and they came to him. He appointed twelve (whom he also named apostles) that they might be with him and he might send them forth to preach and to have authority to drive out demons: (he appointed the twelve:) Simon, whom he named Peter; James, son of Zebedee, and John the brother of James, whom he named Boanerges, that is, sons of thunder; Andrew, Philip, Bartholomew, Matthew, Thomas, James the son of Alphaeus; Thaddeus, Simon the Cananean, and Judas Iscariot who betrayed him.      (Mk 3:13–19)*

The New Testament indicates that this group was chosen early in Jesus' public ministry. This means they spent nearly three years under our Lord's sacred tutelage. The twelve were shaped into a closely knit core that had its source in Jesus. They were always in his company; they witnessed his miracles, saw his virtues, heard his public addresses; they dined, recreated, and, above all, prayed with him. They were the recipients of private instructions to which others were not privy.

This novitiate of "being with Jesus" formed them into a sacred fraternity and prepared them for the insuperable responsibility of evangelizing the world after Jesus' ascension into heaven.[4] When their hour came they proved themselves to have been well trained by the Lord. Strengthened by the experience of Pentecost, they became the primitive cell of a worldwide campaign of evangelization.[5] It is significant that the first propagation of the gospel began with a small but convinced minority of believers.

The apostles, personally prepared and authorized by Christ to be the first fellowship of his evangelizing Church, handed down to subsequent generations what they themselves received from the Lord. Their apostolic communion was the critical mass directly responsible for the spread of the early Church, and their success in extending the kingdom of God was nothing short of miraculous. By the time of the death of the last apostle, St. John, small but vital Christian communities flourished in virtually all of the major cities of the Mediterranean world and even in regions beyond the Roman Empire. The Christian faith had been firmly implanted in Europe and would eventually reach every culture on Earth. As the chosen ambassadors of Christ, the missionary outreach of the apostolic college represents the most dramatic moment of evangelization in Church history.[6]

The paradigm of evangelization revealed in the missionary society of the twelve can be called the Fraternity model. It connotes a company of believers fused together in dynamic unity by the Spirit of Christ and commissioned by him to diffuse his saving gospel to others. It entails the selection, formation, and commissioning of a group of disciples who become a small fellowship, a creative minority, empowered by prayer and sent forth to lead others into the light of Jesus.[7]

The French abbot Jean-Baptiste Chautard captured the essence of this model and described how it works in his classic, *The Soul of the Apostolate*. He explained that the Fraternity model calls for a nucleus of fervent Christians, "shock troops" of evangelization, whose principal aim is to lead others to a profound relationship with Jesus Christ. He noted that it was "by this means...rather than by lectures and apologetics that Christianity developed so rapidly in the first centuries of its history, in spite of the power of its enemies, of prejudices of all sorts, and of the general corruption."[8] He claimed that to achieve this kind of growth, it is necessary to form a core group of zealous Christians who possess the full splendor of the evangelical virtues.

This model of evangelization has emerged in history again and again with the founding of the great religious orders, which have infused new life into the Church's missions and apostolates. But according to Chautard, the modern world especially requires that such teams of evangelists come from the ranks of the laity. *"The most necessary thing of all, at this time, is for every parish to possess a group of laymen who will be at the same time virtuous, enlightened, resolute, and truly apostolic."*[9] Today we fully realize that the laity are called to share in the Church's mission in virtue of their baptism, and that they have their particular role to play in the evangelization and sanctification of humankind.[10] Chautard's exhortation, which he first made in 1907 while living the life of a Cistercian monk, was echoed at Vatican II.

Chautard espoused a three-step plan for this model of evangelization. First, draw from the general populace of Christians a minority of qualified candidates capable of a serious interior life. It poses no problem if the core group is small. Second, develop within the members of this group a profound love for Jesus Christ. Train them in the ways of Christian prayer, meditation, and the evangelical virtues. In the process the Holy Spirit fuses them together into a fraternity. Do not release them for the work of evangelization until they are solidly grounded in the interior life, says the abbot. Third, when they have matured, send forth these lay apostles into the secular domain among their own associates to reap a bountiful harvest for the Lord.

The process of preparation requires personal direction, mentoring, instruction, and encouragement.[11] This community of lay apostles propagates the faith by influencing their peers through personal contact, word, and example in the temporal settings of ordinary human life. In this way they become a creative leaven that spreads concentric waves of faith, hope, and love through society.

Chautard is describing perfectly the Fraternity model of evangelization. He says that this was our Lord's own strategy, and that Jesus himself ushered in the transformation of humankind by means of a select fellowship of twelve evangelists. "The little flock of [apostles] chosen and formed by Christ Himself, and afterwards set on fire by the Holy Spirit, was enough to begin the regeneration of the world." [12]

This method of selecting and forming a core group of fervent laypersons into a zealous team of evangelists is precisely the technique used by St. Philip Neri. He launched this work from San Girolamo Church in the heart of the old city of Rome. In 1564, St. Philip gathered a group of eight or ten young men in his rectory for regular prayer meetings. Each meeting revolved around a regime of silent prayer, spiritual reading, and a religious discourse initiated by St. Philip. The topic of the discourse usually centered on the Gospel of John or the work of one of the great spiritual masters. It was followed by discussion, and concluded with chants. Under his guidance these meetings inflamed the hearts of the young men with a newfound love of God and formed them into a cohesive community.[13]

Soon the number of attendees grew to thirty, and in 1557 the group moved to a larger room, which St. Philip called the "Oratory." Those who attended included day-laborers and tradesmen, as well as scholars, noblemen, and renowned musicians like Giovanni Animuccia and Pierluigi da Palestrina. The quality of the motets and polyphonic works sung at the Oratory attracted artists and the cultured people of Rome.

St. Philip encouraged the devout reception of the sacraments. To increase the young men's fervor, he would assign certain members to make presentations on Church history and the lives of the saints to the rest of the group. The gatherings were gently well ordered and marked by joy, humor, beauty, simplicity, glorious melody, and contagious love.

The members of the Oratory became famous throughout Rome. Eventually this group evolved into a formal community called the Congregation of the Oratory, a society of priests whose purpose is prayer, preaching, and the promotion of the sacramental life. As a source of warmth, humanity, and holiness, the Oratory became a great movement of reform in the post-Reformation Church. The Oratory of St. Philip Neri accurately depicts the nature of the Fraternity model of evangelization: a small but zealous core of believers formed and animated by the Spirit of Christ, and sent forth to evangelize society.

## Example: The Paulist Fathers

Although Chautard emphasized the lay apostolate in his description of the Fraternity model of evangelization, we noted that it was also the evangelical thrust behind the creation of the Church's religious orders and communities. Virtually all of the religious congregations in the Church began as a small core of committed members with a particular charism that evolved into a larger fellowship or community. In American church history, the Fraternity model is typified in the founding and works of the Missionary Society of St. Paul the Apostle, the first religious community of Catholic priests established in the United States. The Paulist Fathers, or Paulists, as they are more popularly called, were founded by Fr. Isaac Thomas Hecker (1819–88) and canonically approved in 1858.

Hecker was born in 1819 in New York to a German immigrant family who owned a bakery. Raised a Methodist, he attended public schools in the city until age thirteen, when he went to work in the family business. In the 1830s, he became involved in a social reform movement that apparently triggered within him serious religious sentiments.[14] In an attempt to come to terms with questions about God and man that fermented within him, he made a diligent search of German philosophy for ultimate solutions.

In 1842, Hecker had a sudden and startling religious experience, an intuitive mystical epiphany, which shook the core of his person. "It was real and genuine with lasting results that altered the entire course of his life."[15]

His friend Orestes Brownson, a colleague he knew from the reform movement, tried to help Hecker sort out the meaning of the experience. Brownson arranged for Hecker to go to Brook Farm in West Roxbury, Massachusetts, in 1843, to join a commune of New England Transcendentalists who were trying to create a utopian community.

Among these Emersonian radicals and romantics, Hecker attempted to comprehend the spiritual experience that had so completely altered his life. In his search, he examined every religious option, including Catholicism. He read Newman's *Tracts for the Times,* and on Easter, to satisfy his curiosity, he visited a Catholic church for the Sunday Mass.

On August 14, 1843, Hecker took leave of Brook Farm. His stay at Roxbury had not yielded the resolution he had sought for his mystical awakening. He returned to his family and resumed his work at the New York bakery. He became more contemplative and sought opportunities for prayer, still longing to respond to a spiritual calling that beckoned within. He explored the Christian denominations of the city, and, like his friend Brownson, Hecker was unconsciously tending toward Rome.

Hecker began to surrender to these vague interior promptings. Then Brownson made a shocking disclosure to Isaac; he had begun instruction to become a Catholic and urged his friend to join him. Hecker was bewildered and became afflicted with a severe disquiet of soul.

On June 8, 1844, thanks to the intercession of Brownson, he was able to discuss his interior dispositions with Bishop Fitzpatrick, the auxiliary of Boston. This visit dispelled his doubts, and he took the "serious, sacred, sincere, solemn step" to become Catholic.[16] His decision was accompanied by such perfect peace that no external circumstances could deter his resolve. On August 2, 1844, Hecker made his profession of faith before Bishop McCloskey of New York at Old St. Patrick's Cathedral on Mott Street. The next day he returned to the cathedral and made a general confession.

Hecker continued his work at the bakery and the next year passed slowly. A higher calling persisted and, with the help of Bishop McCloskey, he became convinced that he was called to the priesthood and was led to the Congregation of the Most Holy Redeemer. In July 1845, he crossed the Atlantic to study for the priesthood with the Redemptorists in Belgium.

During his Redemptorist novitiate, he found that the lives and writings of the saints, as well as the workings of divine grace, had enabled him finally to comprehend the religious experience of his youth.[17] Roman Catholic spirituality and theology became the key that unlocked for him the personal mystery he had sought to understand since his Brook Farm days.

Within a few months of this clarification in Europe, a new development took root in his soul. Hecker became seized with a growing desire to convert America to Catholicism. He wrote to his mother that when he returned home he would labor "for the conversion of our country."[18] This developing aspect of his vocation led him to conclude that hidden within the seed of his own conversion was a providential grace for all of America. His passionate belief that "the Catholic Church is the ideal of every individual of the race and the universal ideal of humanity"[19] was solidified during his time in Europe.

Hecker did not wait until his return home to initiate his mission to the United States. He began writing letters to his family and friends back home, including one to Henry Thoreau in 1849, urging them to embrace Christ fully by entering the Roman Catholic Church.

Hecker was transferred to the Redemptorist house in London in August 1848, and was ordained a priest there on October 23, 1849, by Cardinal Wiseman. On March 19, 1851, at the age of thirty-one, he returned to the United States. He was immediately incorporated into a Redemptorist mission band assigned to preach parish revivals across the nation.

The newly ordained Redemptorist knew the true purpose of his life, the answer to the question that had tormented him for so many years, lay in a specific mission to evangelize American Protestants. Hecker was convinced that, like himself, Americans who sincerely searched for God would, with the proper direction, find him in the living experience of the Catholic Church. As individual Americans made this discovery, it would snowball into the wholesale conversion of the nation to Catholicism.[20]

Hecker formally began his outreach to Protestants in 1857 at the end of a Catholic parish mission in Virginia. He held a series of public lectures in which he presented the tenets of Catholicism in a positive, engaging manner that appealed to the general sensibilities of the American spirit. He held similar gatherings in New Jersey and Connecticut.[21] He also began a writing campaign, authoring *Questions of the Soul* (1855) and *Aspirations of Nature* (1857), apologetical works written in his typically persuasive style, to explain the truths of Catholicism to the American public. Hecker's approach to evangelizing "was quite personal; his conversion became a paradigm for his ministry and the prototype of a new American Catholicism."[22] He became a prominent American figure in the eyes of both Catholics and Protestants.

As his outreach to non-Catholics became the centerpiece of his ministry, he became dissatisfied with the limitations the Redemptorists placed on his heartfelt mission to the Protestants. Although the last night of a standard parish mission was designed to encourage Catholic attendees to bring a Protestant friend, this was not enough for Hecker. He wanted a specific, comprehensive outreach aimed at non-Catholics.

A conflict ensued, as the Redemptorist leadership believed that their first priority should be to the German-speaking Catholic immigrants, while Hecker wanted to devote himself entirely to non-Catholics. Hecker made an appeal to the Redemptorist superior general in Rome, which backfired. The tension swelled, and Hecker, together with four like-minded Redemptorists, obtained a papal release from the Redemptorist congregation, and encouragement from Pius IX to establish their own community. In July 1858, the Archbishop of New York, John Hughes, approved their rule of life.

Their little fellowship, the Missionary Society of St. Paul the Apostle, became a congregation of secular priests living a communal life with the mission of evangelizing non-Catholic Americans. Hecker was elected the superior of the new community. Hughes gave the newborn community charge of a new parish near Central Park. The fathers named their parish St. Paul the Apostle; it became a center of evangelization that would reach out to all parts of the country.

St. Paul's parish was organized as a perpetual mission, where the superior quality of preaching, liturgy, and music was intended to enhance the spirituality of Catholics and inspire non-Catholics to examine Catholicism. The strategy worked, and many from throughout the city flocked to St. Paul's. One New York newspaper reported that "wonders" were taking place at St. Paul's, and that there was standing room only on Sundays; the preaching was so effective that nearby saloons were closing.[23] The Paulists also continued their circuit of parish missions throughout the country.

Recruitment to the new congregation was slow, but gradually new members joined. The operation of the parish, the promotion of parish missions, the training of new recruits, and the raising of funds were all a heavy burden for the small community. For a while this workload, which primarily served Catholics, kept Hecker and his men from the purpose for which they were established: the conversion of America to Catholicism. It was nevertheless mandatory to lay this foundation if the Paulists were one day going to launch their true mission. Hecker's conviction that America was ripe for conversion had not waned; he believed it was imminent.

The Paulist founder resumed his lecture tours and missions to non-Catholics in 1862. In New Haven, Connecticut, over three thousand people jammed the local music hall and hundreds had to be turned away. In this manner he worked the big cities in the Northeast and the Midwest. Unfortunately, this project did not produce many new Catholics. It required vigilant follow-up work that the local priests and parishes were unable or unwilling to do.

Hecker acknowledged that these lectures were not producing the desired fruit. In a creative new response he launched the *Catholic World,* an eclectic periodical designed to explain the Catholic faith in a nondefensive manner. The magazine was also intended to awaken the Catholic clergy and laity to a more zealous and penetrating appreciation of their own tradition. Following on the heels of this endeavor, Hecker established a Catholic publication society to produce short, inexpensive pamphlets on points of faith, for broad and easy distribution. This institution eventually became Paulist Press.

All the while, Hecker's confreres supported him in these works; this small but zealous band of men also administrated St. Paul's parish, and answered many requests for parish missions. These activities were only the preliminary steps toward the ultimate vision he and his fellow Paulists had for the United States of America: "a future Catholic Christian commonwealth [that] when converted, [would see] all Americans…acknowledge the presence of God in their own hearts, in the Church, and in history."[24]

With experience, Hecker had come to understand that the process of making America a truly Christian nation required not only the conversion of non-Catholics to the fullness of the faith but also of Catholics, who as yet did not entirely realize their blessings and responsibility before God.

In 1866, Hecker addressed the bishops of the United States at the Second Plenary Council in Baltimore. Standing at the pulpit of the beautiful Baltimore Cathedral, Hecker enjoined the bishops to take up the task of converting America:

> Nowhere is there a promise of a brighter future for the Church
> than in our own country. Here, thanks to our American
> Constitution, the Church is free to do her divine work. Here,

she finds a civilization in harmony with her divine teachings. Here, Christianity is promised a reception from an intelligent and free people, that will bring forth a development of unprecedented glory. For religion is never so beautiful as when in connection with knowledge and freedom.[25]

Hecker saw a perfect match between the American civil spirit and Catholic Christianity. American culture was a fertile bed waiting to flower forth into a new Catholic synthesis. He believed all that was needed was the redemption and sanctification of this enlightened civil society by the plentitude of divine truth.

Between December 1869 and September 1870, Hecker was a participant in Vatican I. After the council, he continued to travel in Europe over the next few years and also visited Palestine and Egypt. In 1875, he returned to New York and turned most of his attention to strengthening the Society of St. Paul the Apostle and building up the *Catholic World*. At this point in his life he did not have a high public profile. His health deteriorated, and on December 22, 1888, he passed over to the next life in the presence of his Paulist brothers. Services were held at St. Paul's church and the story was well covered by the popular press.

Paulist Fr. Walter Elliott wrote Hecker's biography after his death. It was well accepted in the United States, but an introduction to the abridged French translation caused a conflict in Europe between liberal and conservative theologians. The controversy alarmed the Vatican, and Leo XIII intervened with the encyclical letter *Testem Benevolentiae*. This letter was addressed to the American bishops and condemned a number of liberal ideas with which the name of Isaac Hecker had been associated. Specifically, the encyclical denounced the notion that Catholic teaching should be softened in favor of attracting converts; that the Holy Spirit was manifesting himself in a new way in the modern era; that spiritual direction for laypersons had lost its importance; that more emphasis should be placed on the active virtues rather than the contemplative life; and that the nature of Catholicism in America might be different from Catholicism in the rest of the world. These views were grouped together under the term *Americanism*.

The encyclical had a chilling effect on the liberal party in the Church in America. The Paulists held that these ideas, the "heresy of Americanism," were a distortion of Hecker's real positions and in fact a "phantom heresy," but the entire incident cast a shadow over his reputation.[26]

Despite this setback, the Paulists continued to grow. They established new houses and took responsibility for parishes in Chicago and Oregon. The Paulists also ventured into campus ministry at non-Catholic colleges.[27] Paulist Fr. Walter Elliot attempted to reestablish the lecture series to non-Catholics. In 1893, he spoke in public halls across Michigan and, in 1894, repeated the process in Ohio. Elliot also helped to found the Catholic Missionary Union in 1896. Its purpose was to sponsor conferences to promote and plan the evangelization of the United States. It was also intended to develop missionary awareness on the diocesan level, and to publish the monthly journal *The Missionary*.[28]

At the turn of the twentieth century, the Paulists concentrated less energy on parish missions and emphasized the training of Catholic evangelists. A house of studies was opened at the Catholic University of America in 1902 and staffed by Paulist priests. Here the congregation offered a training program for diocesan priests specially designed to prepare them for outreach to non-Catholic Americans. The net effect of Elliot's leadership was to shift the emphasis from the making of converts to the recruitment and development of convert makers.[29]

In 1943, the Paulists began a new apostolic venture: the Catholic Information Center. Fr. John T. McGinn was the visionary of this innovation. The first center germinated in Toronto, and then others were opened in New York, Boston, Baltimore, Los Angeles, and Grand Rapids. The downtown information center was open to the public and built around an inquiry class aimed at non-Catholics, although Catholics also attended. Catholic literature and informal hospitality were also features of this apostolate.[30] During these years the Paulists attempted to enlighten the Catholic clergy and laity about their missionary responsibility.

In the second half of the twentieth century, the society's printing house, Paulist Press, moved from the publication of periodicals and pamphlets to paperback and hardbound books.[31] Paulist Press helped to meet the need for new publications that were in demand after Vatican II.

As the Paulist Society moved into the post-conciliar era, Paulist Fr. Alvin Illig took the lead by devising a program of parish-based evangelization in 1973. It included door-to-door visitation, a direct-phone campaign, and local public advertising. The target of this effort was the vast field of fallen-away Catholics and the unchurched. This model was adopted by the bishops of the United States, and, with their collaboration, Illig launched a national evangelization program intended to reach the nation's unchurched Americans. The Paulist National Catholic Evangelization Association was established in Washington as a national center to direct this program and to coordinate the evangelization of the country at every level. In 1976, Illig was invited by the American bishops to become the first director of a national office for Catholic evangelization.[32] Today the Paulists continue to be the nation's leaders in this ministry.

## Isaac Hecker and the Paulist Fathers Evaluated

In a letter he sent to a missionary in Louisiana one year after the founding of the Paulists, Hecker wrote:

> The conversion of the American people to the Catholic faith has ripened into a conviction with me which lies beyond the region of doubt. My life, my labours, and my death is [*sic*] consecrated to it. No other aim as an end outside of my own salvation and perfection can occupy my attention a moment...In the union of Catholic faith and American civilization a new birth awaits them all, and a future for the Church brighter than any past. That is briefly my "Credo."[33]

Today, of course, the United States is 22 percent Catholic. It does not appear that the proportion of Catholics in the nation has been significantly affected as a result of the work of Hecker and his associates. Are we to infer from this statistic that Hecker and the Paulists have failed? Considering the many accomplishments of Hecker and his companions since the establishment of the Paulist Society, one resists this conclusion. The founding of a religious community, the first congregation of priests in America no less, is a prodigious achievement in any reckoning of Church history. The Paulist Fathers count 150 members today, all of whom are dedicated to the evangelization of America. This fact alone makes Hecker's work a triumph of faith.

The many innovations initiated by Hecker and his disciples, like town meetings, campus ministry at non-Catholic colleges, training programs and centers for evangelists, and downtown information centers, are great monuments of missionary zeal. The congregation's publishing house, Paulist Press, is a ranking Catholic publisher today. The Paulists' overall leadership in evangelization signified by the Paulist National Catholic Evangelization Association, and the congregation's intimate collaboration with the American bishops in this apostolate, are additional evidences of success.

Even amid the controversies surrounding the accusations of Americanism, Hecker's appreciation of the dynamics of inculturation, that is, the Spirit-guided dialectic between Catholicism and American civil values in the process of evangelization, indicates the foresight of this apostle. The same can be said of his insistence upon the need for both non-Catholics and Catholics to be converted to the fullness of Christ's revelation. Also, echoing the sentiments of Vatican II, Hecker believed that Catholicism, when it was proposed honestly, reasonably, and charitably, was inherently attractive and compelling.

The conversion of America to the Catholic faith has not yet been realized, but the Church's efforts to evangelize the nation have become almost synonymous with the work of the Paulist congregation. Starting as a band of five, the Paulists have evolved into the right arm of the nation's bishops in the mission of evangelizing the United States. "What began with Isaac Hecker speaking as a single voice [has] now become the stated pastoral task of the American Church."[34] In the work of the Missionary Society of St. Paul, America has been the beneficiary of one of the enduring examples of the Fraternity model of evangelization, which to this day continues to promote the mission of its founder.

In these days since Vatican II, what are we to say today of Hecker's essential goal? What are we to think of Hecker's aspiration to convert Protestant Christians to Catholicism? Is such a goal valid in an ecumenical age, or even possible in America's pluralistic society today? Have the documents of Vatican II had the cumulative effect of causing Catholics to consider such an aspiration with ambivalence?

The answers to these questions "all depend," says Benedict XVI, "on the correct interpretation of the council or—as we would say today—on its proper hermeneutics, the correct key to its interpretation and application."[35] There are two competing hermeneutics of Vatican II that have been quarrelling with each other since 1962. There is "a hermeneutic of discontinuity and rupture," which has frequently been trumpeted by the mass media and also advanced by one trend in modern theology. Contrariwise, there is the "'hermeneutic of reform,' of renewal in the continuity of the one subject-Church which the Lord has given to us."[36]

The hermeneutic of discontinuity pushes for a divergence or cleavage between the pre-conciliar and post-conciliar Church. According to this interpretation "it is not necessary to follow the texts of the Council but its spirit."[37] The council itself is to be understood "as a sort of constituent that eliminates an old constitution and creates a new one." Of course, the council "Fathers had no such mandate and no one had ever given them one; nor could anyone have given them one because the essential constitution of the Church comes from the Lord and was given to us so that we might attain eternal life and, starting from this perspective, be able to illuminate life in time and time itself."[38]

Conversely, the hermeneutic of reform offers the key to an authentic interpretation of Vatican II. John XXIII, in his address on October 11, 1962, which opened the council, presented this hermeneutic as the proper way to understand Vatican II. He said,

> [the Council wished] to transmit the doctrine, pure and integral, without any attenuation or distortion...to guard this precious treasure...which however should be studied and expounded through the methods of research and through the literary forms of modern thought. The substance of the ancient doctrine of the deposit of faith is one thing, and the way in which it is presented is another.[39]

The council called not for a departure but for a new and vital relationship of this eternal truth with contemporary thinking and modern exigencies. The council hoped for a positive and fruitful engagement with modernism rather than the condemnations that emerged from "the clash between the Church's faith and a radical liberalism" witnessed in the days of Pius IX.[40] The Church had to address the relationship between the faith and modern science both natural and historical; the Church and the state; and finally the problem of religious intolerance. Arriving at solutions to these questions precipitated a discontinuity on contingent matters. It "even corrected certain historical decisions, but in this apparent discontinuity [the council] has actually preserved and deepened [the Church's] inmost nature and true identity."[41]

The hermeneutic of continuity, then, provides the correct key for understanding the council, which is pertinent to our original question: Is Isaac Hecker's desire to lead everyone to the Catholic Church valid today? Benedict XVI summarizes the response: "The Church, both before and after the Council, was and is the same Church, one, holy, catholic and apostolic, journeying on through time,"[42] proclaiming the fullness of God's truth in season and out of season. Hecker wrote to Henry David Thoreau on May 15, 1847: "The Catholic church is the ideal of every individual of the race and the universal ideal of humanity."[43] A careful reading of the documents of Vatican II, with the hermeneutic of reform and continuity, indicates that from the Church's perspective, Hecker's words are as valid today as they were when he wrote them to Thoreau in the nineteenth century.

We can also surmise from his life and statements that Hecker would have greatly appreciated the ecumenical inroads that have been paved by Vatican II. Hecker the evangelist would have agreed with Benedict XVI, John Paul II, and Paul VI that the proclamation of the gospel is impaired by the lack of unity among Christians. "The power of evangelization will find itself considerably diminished if those who proclaim the Gospel are divided among themselves in all sorts of ways."[44]

The fact is, the work of evangelization and the work of ecumenism are inextricably bound together. The quest for Christian unity is not merely an internal matter for the Christian communities. "It is a matter of the love which God has in Jesus Christ for all humanity; to stand in the way of this love is an offense against him and against his plan to gather all people in Christ."[45] John Paul II was convinced of the connection between Christian unity and the success of the Church's mission to evangelize. He returned to this theme many times during his pontificate. He once expressed his thoughts on this issue in these words:

When I say that for me, as Bishop of Rome, the ecumenical task is "one of the pastoral priorities" of my Pontificate, I think of the grave obstacle which the lack of unity represents for the proclamation of the Gospel. A Christian Community which believes in Christ and desires, with Gospel fervour, the salvation of mankind can hardly be closed to the promptings of the Holy Spirit, who leads all Christians towards full and visible unity. Here an imperative of charity is in question, an imperative which admits of no exception.[46]

The complexities of achieving this unity are beyond the scope of this study, but one thing is certain, today every true evangelist must appreciate the value of the ecumenical movement.

## The Fraternity Model Today

Without prejudice to the importance of religious congregations like the Paulist Fathers in the work of evangelization, Vatican II recognized the laity as indispensable in the execution of the Church's mission, as did Chautard. The Fraternity model of evangelization is especially suited for enlisting the collaboration of the laity for this task.

Paul VI advanced the concept of small lay communities in the context of evangelizing the modern world. He said that "they spring from the need to live the Church's life more intensely, or from the desire and quest for a more human dimension such as larger ecclesial communities can offer only with difficulty."[47] These communities often have a sociological basis, linking people together of similar age, culture, social status, or profession. The members of these groups are searching for a deeper experience of faith, worship, fraternal charity, and prayer. They aspire to opportunities for apostolic service, or to promote a Christian cause.

On the parish level in North America, these associations of committed laypersons have assumed a variety of forms, for example, Bible study groups, prayer groups, rosary groups, faith-sharing groups, pro-life groups, Legion of Mary praesidia, social action groups, and the like. These small communities are immensely important in advancing the work of evangelization, for both individuals and the culture in which they are immersed.

As Chautard said, *"the most necessary thing of all, at this time, is for every parish to possess a group of laymen [and laywomen] who will be at the same time virtuous, enlightened, resolute and apostolic."*[48] This exhortation encourages pastors to initiate the work of evangelization on the parish level through the formation of small communities of trusted co-workers who will help them in the various tasks of spreading the gospel.

This method is easily implemented and can be done immediately with a minimum of resources. The pastor, or even the associate pastor or deacon, has multiple opportunities to select a core group of collaborators from within the ranks of his parishioners. Then he has only to train them in Christian spirituality and the apostolate, and charge them to be responsive to the needs of the Church and society.

Today it is even possible for the laity themselves to form a community committed to the work of the Church. Since Vatican II there has been a proliferation of lay associations and ecclesial groups that have been formed for charitable and religious purposes. The right of the laity to initiate these groups is essential to the life and mission of the Church. Their primary and proper sphere of influence is in the temporal order—the world of politics, society, economics, culture, arts and sciences, international life, the family, education of children and young people, professional work, and suffering.[49] These committed lay groups have the potential to make great contributions to reviving parish life and "reawaken[ing] missionary zeal towards non-believers and believers themselves who have abandoned the faith or grown lax in the Christian life."[50]

To be effective, these associations must maintain a harmonious and respectful relationship with Church authorities. The basic criteria for maintaining ecclesial unity with the local church is explained by John Paul II.

First, the lay association must emphasize the primacy of the call to holiness of every baptized person and lead others to this goal. Second, it must profess the Catholic faith in its totality and always in conformity with the teaching office of the Church. Third, it should witness to a strong and sincere fidelity to the papacy and strive to preserve an obedient and cordial relationship with the local bishop. The community should maintain an esteem and appreciation for all expressions of the Christian apostolate.

Fourth, the lay association has to conform to and participate in the Church's universal mission of evangelization and sanctification of humankind. Fifth, it must be committed to advancing a just and loving society. Finally, the lay group should show forth in its life a renewed appreciation for prayer, for the Church's liturgy, and for vocations to Christian marriage, the priesthood, and religious life.

These criteria provide the parameters for discerning an ecclesial lay community that is capable of being a true source of missionary fruitfulness.[51] When lay associations carry out their apostolate in this manner, they reflect the Fraternity model of evangelization as lived by the twelve apostles and described by Chautard.

No matter what configuration the Fraternity model assumes, it excels in providing a method to initiate evangelization promptly, even if the resources and personnel are scant. It also enables Christians who are at a loss as to how to begin the work of evangelization with a concrete point of departure, especially when the standard local structures do not seem to offer such an opportunity. The method is simple and adaptable, and requires only a little zeal on the part of three, two, or perhaps even one person, to get started.

## Considerations for Christian Education

In the New Testament, "among the many images that Jesus utilized for the new people—flock, wedding guests, plantation, God's building, God's city—one stands out as his favorite, that of the family of God."[52] This theme of Christian community is central to the gospel. Educators today appreciate this and realize that Christian fraternity by its very nature is an instrument for introducing people to the love of Christ.[53]

In our technological age many individuals are overcome by a sense of isolation and estrangement. Small, vital fraternities offer unique possibilities for befriending others in Christ and giving them a sense of belonging and solidarity among themselves and with the Church. Such experiences draw people to the source of this brotherhood where they find the Lord. Forums of social support and fraternity, imbued with genuine faith, build people up and help them to open their hearts to God and others. The

Christian community itself educates individuals in the mystery of human and divine intimacy.

Our earlier analysis of Hecker's mission raises another facet of the fraternal bond of Christians: the question of the universal family of Christ, or the unity of all Christian believers. As Benedict XVI says, no one who is concerned about the Christian faith can evade the ecumenical aspect of propagating the gospel.[54] A desire for Christian unity should be the aspiration of every Christian. This concern points out to the catechist the importance of learning and teaching about the different churches and ecclesial communities that profess faith in Christ. John Paul II also linked "theological discussion…cooperation in works of charity, and above all the ecumenism of holiness," as part of the Catholic Church's plan of evangelization for the third millennium.[55]

Precisely how this movement toward Christian unity is to unfold in its far-reaching dimensions is not clear. As Benedict XVI stated,

> The formula that the great ecumenists have invented is that we go forward together. It's not a matter of our wanting to achieve certain processes of integration, but we hope that the Lord will awaken people's faith everywhere in such a way that it overflows from one to the other, and the one Church is there. As Catholics, we are persuaded that the basic shape of this one Church is given us in the Catholic Church, but that she is moving toward the future and will allow herself to be educated and led by the Lord. In that sense we do not picture for ourselves any particular model of integration, but simply look to march on in faith under the leadership of the Lord—who knows the way. And in whom we trust.[56]

The religious educator does not have to be an expert in these matters to support the venture of creating a spirit of fraternity with other Christians.

This discourse with other Christians cannot be the extent of the Catholic mission of fraternal charity and dialogue. Religious pluralism is a fact of life in America and throughout the world. We must also extend ourselves to Jews, Muslims, Hindus, Buddhists, and followers of traditional religions. In this regard, Christians engage their brothers and sisters of other religions in respectful dialogue. Catholics wish to learn about their beliefs and share with them the fullness of God's revelation and love.

The Church sees no conflict between proclaiming Christ and inter-religious dialogue; rather, it is part of her mission. In these fraternal exchanges, says Benedict XVI, the Church is not speaking to someone about something that is entirely unknown to him or her; it is opening up the depth that is hidden in that person's own religion. This process enables the one who proclaims Christ to be also a receiver, listening to and desiring to penetrate the mystery of the Logos ever more deeply.[57]

While the Church gladly acknowledges whatever is true and holy in non-Christian religions, "this does not lessen her duty and resolve to proclaim without fail Jesus Christ who is 'the way, and the truth, and the life.'"[58] Everyone has a right to hear this truth, including non-Christians,[59] because religious "pluralism does not exist for its own sake; it *is directed to the fullness of truth.*"[60] When members of the Church enter into this kind of exchange, they address people of other religions with full respect for their freedom. Christians do not *impose* the gospel on others; rather they *propose* the fullness of God's self-revelation. They do this while respecting individuals and cultures, and honoring the sanctuary of their conscience.[61] These points are significant for anyone employed in the ministry of religious education. [62]

# CHAPTER V

# THE AREOPAGUS MODEL

## Inculturation

*The Areopagus model depicts the effort to transform every stratum of a given culture or people into a Christ-centered society. It claims St. Paul's discourse at the Areopagus as its prototype. St. Paul's apology in Acts 17:16–34 is the paradigm of the encounter of the gospel with human culture.*

## The Areopagus Model Defined

Although the golden age of Athens had passed by the time of Christ's incarnation, this celebrated city continued to be admired in the Mediterranean world when St. Paul arrived there in AD 52. Its prosperity was still evident and Greek culture, art, and learning preserved their superiority.[1] The Athens of the first century AD also retained much of its surpassing physical beauty. The temples, the gymnasia, the theaters, the libraries, and the colonnaded markets all harkened back to the days of grandeur.

This was the city that St. Paul visited, almost by accident, after he was expelled from Beroea and on his way to Corinth. When he broached the city limits of Athens, it was only two decades after our Lord's ascension. This capital of classical antiquity was untouched by Christianity prior to the apostle's arrival. As St. Paul waited for Silas and Timothy to catch up with him from Beroea, he explored the city.

At a glance the polytheism of the Athenians was apparent. St. Paul came upon pagan shrines and statues at every turn. Sacrifices were offered to the gods in these temples. Side by side with the ancient Greek worship, the more secretive mystery religions and Orphic cults also flourished. St. Paul reacted to the idolatry vehemently. He also challenged Epicurean and Stoic philosophers in the Agora, the principal marketplace of Athens. Some Greeks dismissed him as a noisy chatterbox. Others alleged that he was *a promoter of foreign gods* (v. 19).

St. Paul caused a sensation in Athens, but the Athenians prided themselves in being open-minded, were accustomed to debate, and eagerly welcomed these occasions. So they arranged for St. Paul to speak at the Areopagus, where he could make a formal presentation of his new teaching.

The Areopagus was a great Athenian courthouse on the hill of Mars across from the Acropolis where the supreme council and court of Athens used to convene.[2] It is not clear whether St. Paul spoke to the council or was merely taken to the Areopagus so that his argument could be better heard. After the Athenians assembled,

> *Then Paul stood up at the Areopagus and said: "You Athenians, I see that in every respect you are very religious. For as I walked around looking carefully at your shrines, I even discovered an altar inscribed, 'To an Unknown God.' What therefore you unknowingly worship, I proclaim to you. The God who made the world and all that is in it, the Lord of heaven and earth, does not dwell in sanctuaries made by human hands, nor is he served by human hands because he needs anything. Rather it is he who gives to everyone life and breath and everything. He made from one the whole human race to dwell on the entire surface of the earth, and he fixed the ordered seasons and the boundaries of their regions, so that people might seek God, even perhaps grope for him and find him, though indeed he is not far from any one of us. For 'In him we live and move and have our being,' as even some of your poets have said, 'For we too are his offspring.' Since therefore we are the offspring of God, we ought not to think that the divinity is like an image fashioned from gold, silver, or stone by human art and imagination. God has overlooked the times of ignorance, but now he demands that all people everywhere repent because he has established a day on which he will 'judge the world with justice' through a man*

*he has appointed, and he has provided confirmation for all by raising*
*him from the dead."* (Acts 17:22–31)

No doubt St. Paul wished to speak at length, but those assembled broke off the hearing once he introduced the concept of resurrection from the dead.[3] Some sneered, others evaded him, saying that they would listen to him again on another occasion. But his efforts were not altogether ineffective. Remarkably, this abbreviated exhortation, the first formal announcement of the gospel uttered in Athens, produced converts. *Among them were Dionysius, a member of the Court of the Areopagus, a woman named Damaris, and others with them* (v. 34). Tradition holds that Dionysius, known as the Areopagite, would later become a bishop and die a martyr's death.[4]

This passage from the Acts of the Apostles is acknowledged as one of the great moments in the history of evangelization.[5] In this discourse St. Paul "enters into 'dialogue' with the cultural and religious values" of the Athenians.[6] He engages them on the level of their indigenous values and terminology and compliments their religiosity. In his reference to the transcendence of God, he incorporates Greek philosophy into his address. The apostle does not attempt to re-create their philosophy; rather, "he recognizes it as a legitimate conversation partner in the approach to God."[7] At the climax of his speech St. Paul even appeals to Greek literature for his purposes by quoting one of their poets.

If we consider the surpassing quality of Greek culture in the ancient world, says John Paul II, "we will understand that this speech by Paul can be considered the very symbol of the encounter of the Gospel with human culture."[8] He appealed to the inchoate longings of an exceptionally cultured people, by means of their own cultural reference points, in order to lead them to Christ.

Catholic historian Christopher Dawson recognizes St. Paul's strategy of inculturation. He points out that St. Paul put to the service of the gospel the intellectual formation he had received in Tarsus, a celebrated city of learning and culture itself: "St. Paul was by no means unconscious of the value of humane letters in the work of evangelization. In fact he was himself the first Christian humanist, and his speech to the Athenians, with its appeal to the Hellenistic doctrines of the unity of the human race, of divine providence and of the natural affinity between the human and divine natures, is the basic document of Christian humanism."[9]

The seed of Christianity St. Paul sowed in Athens and elsewhere would bear great fruit, but it would take time. Centuries of dialectical exchange between classical culture and the gospel first had to transpire from these encounters. Eventually this dialogue blossomed into a synthesis of Christianity and Hellenism that transformed Europe into a Christian society.[10] From the earliest days, evangelization and inculturation became inseparable colleagues.

St. Paul's address to the Athenians is a seminal model of inculturation. This episode illustrates that the inculturation of the gospel in society is a phenomenon of gradual transformation in Christ. It is the process whereby the mystery of Jesus is proclaimed to a specific culture according to the unique language, ideas, values, customs, traditions, social institutions, art, and philosophy of that culture. Starting with the *semina verba,* the seed of belief, hidden within the culture itself, this encounter with the Christian faith regenerates and transforms the values of the people from within. As the culture is penetrated with the gospel, the light of revelation becomes incarnate in the societal life of the people, purifying it of elements incompatible with the Word of God. At the same time, without adulterating the gospel message, this process of inculturation co-penetrates the Church with worthy elements from the culture being evangelized, and produces a new expression of Christian culture.

Inculturation works, then, in two directions: one is the impact the gospel has on the culture of the people being evangelized; the other is the corresponding effect on the Church that results from its interaction with the new culture. This dynamic led H. Richard Niebuhr to observe that "the problem of culture is therefore the problem of its conversion, not of its replacement by a new creation; though the conversion is so radical that it amounts to a kind of rebirth."[11]

In this process of inculturation three stages can be identified.[12] The first stage is the introduction of Christianity into a culture and the formation of a new group of believers in a given cultural arena. This requires evangelists to learn about the new culture with a discerning degree of openness and receptivity, so that they may translate the gospel into terms accessible to the people they address.

The second stage is that of transformation. This occurs when it is evident that the local church has acquired the knowledge and ability to communicate the Christian message to the new culture on various levels. In this stage a long process of discernment, purification, and the development of new expressions of the deposit of faith emerges. Eventually, a harmony is reached at the local level between fidelity to the received teachings of Christianity and the culture of its people. The result is a cultural synthesis animated by the values of the gospel.

In the third stage, this fresh cultural expression of Christianity becomes a new ecclesial communion bound to the body of Christ through authentic faith and worship. This new communion, in turn, enriches the Church universal with its own cultural uniqueness.

These stages of inculturation can be recognized in the implantation of the Church in the Greek world of the early centuries AD. The movement of inculturation begins with the preaching of St. Paul and the apostles in Asia Minor and Greece and the establishment of communities of believers in the major urban centers of Ephesus, Antioch, Alexandria, and other places like those mentioned in the book of Revelation. Then a far-reaching synthesis of Christianity and Hellenism evolved. This synthesis matured in the East during the patristic age of the fourth and fifth centuries. Finally, a new culture, Byzantine Christianity, emerged. It was marked by a distinct liturgy and the writings of the Eastern church fathers. This new Christian culture also marked the Church's universal definitions of the faith through the christological councils of Nicaea, Constantinople, Ephesus, and Chalcedon.

The transformation was not always smooth. It often erupted into conflicts, riots, and martyrdoms. From personal experience missionaries like St. Paul were aware that in the dialect between Christ and culture, the Church had to be willing to fulfill her prophetic function when necessary. The effort to appeal to cultures can never undermine the gospel's demand to oppose and resist those elements of society marred by sin. When she exercises her prophetic role in this process, we find that there are times when the Church is not so much inculturated as counter-culturated.[13]

As we have seen, St. Paul's address at the Areopagus is the paradigm of gospel inculturation, especially in the first stage of the process. He takes as his point of departure the cultural matrix of his listeners. In this case it was the natural knowledge of God extant in the Greek mindset and the universal longing for spiritual fulfillment fermenting within every person. He uses these as means of preparing the Athenians to receive the fullness of divine revelation.[14] St. Paul's method of engaging those he wished to convert on the level of their own culture is a timeless model of evangelization. In the same way, Christians who desire to proclaim the good news to others in our time "must be attentive to their cultures and their ways of communicating, without allowing the Gospel message to be altered or its meaning or scope diminished."[15]

St. Paul's technique at the Areopagus invites today's evangelists to enter into respectful dialogue with their contemporaries. Like St. Paul, the modern apostle has first to reach out to individuals in familiar terms, precisely where they are, with their particular worries and questions, doubts and fears. Then it becomes possible to help them find the moral and spiritual lights they need to live the fullness of life here and hereafter. Following the Areopagus paradigm, modern evangelists should strive to enter into the very mind and life of the people, paying close attention to the cultural milieu in which they are immersed so as to reach into the hearts of those with whom they dialogue. There is no better way to communicate the message of Christ.[16]

## Example: John Lancaster Spalding

In his day, John Lancaster Spalding (1840–1916) was a providential model of Christian inculturation. His life and work are emblematic of the synthesis of Catholicism and the American spirit that was flourishing at the turn of the twentieth century.

From the beginning, Spalding's world was permeated with the American experience. He was nurtured in the cradle of American culture, having descended from two pioneer families sharing a long history in the American heartland. He was born at the Spalding homestead in Lebanon, Kentucky, on June 2, 1840, the oldest of nine children.[17] His early years were happy. When John was only eight years old, his uncle, Martin Spalding, after a brilliant career in Rome, was consecrated as coadjutor bishop to the saintly Benedict Flaget, the first bishop of Bardstown, Kentucky.[18]

John received all of his education from Catholic schools and institutions. In 1852, at the age of twelve, he was sent for a serious education to

St. Mary's College near Lebanon, where he excelled.[19] Late in the summer of 1857, John headed east to Mount Saint Mary's College and Seminary in Emmitsburg, Maryland. In January 1858, he was sent home, along with some other students, for an unknown infraction involving some contraband in the boys' desks.[20] Humbled by the incident, John continued his studies at a school close to home.

At the age of eighteen, John made up his mind to pursue a vocation to the priesthood. In the meantime, his uncle had been appointed ordinary of Louisville. Uncle Martin had great influence upon his young nephew John's vocational plans and deliberations. At Martin's direction, John was sent to study for the priesthood at Mount Saint Mary's of the West in Cincinnati, where he graduated as valedictorian in 1859.

Bishop Spalding then sent his nephew John to the Catholic University of Louvain in Belgium. The young Kentuckian was pleased with the experience and program of studies at Louvain. This time proved to be the most rewarding period of his life as a student. He was ordained a priest on December 19, 1863, in Malines and completed his license in sacred theology in 1864.

John visited Germany for a few months and then proceeded south to Rome, where his uncle wanted him to spend a year studying "the antiquities [and] perfect[ing] himself in theology by attending the lectures."[21] In June of that same year John's uncle was appointed archbishop of Baltimore. In Rome, John turned to the study of canon law.

John wrote to his uncle and told the archbishop that he left it up to him as to whether he would return to the States as a priest for Baltimore or Louisville. In September 1865, Peter J. Lavialle was ordained bishop of Louisville; he was not inclined to release John to Baltimore; so his uncle did not press for the transfer. John returned to Kentucky a month after General Lee's surrender to General Grant at Appomattox on April 9, 1865.

Between 1865 and his episcopal ordination in 1877, John had little time to devote to the intellectual work to which he was attracted. He was appointed the assistant of Assumption Cathedral in Louisville and secretary to Bishop Lavialle. Lavialle died of a rather sudden illness in 1868, and William G. McCloskey succeeded him as bishop of Louisville. John continued as McCloskey's secretary for a few years and then served as diocesan chancellor and editor of the diocesan newspaper. He was also the founding pastor of St. Augustine's Church, the first parish in Louisville for black Catholics. In addition, Bishop McCloskey put him in charge of the cathedral school.

After Martin Spalding died in 1872, John moved to New York City with his bishop's permission to write a biography of his uncle. He remained in New York, and there his long-standing concern began to emerge: a desire to advance the intellectual life and stature of American Catholics. In 1876, Spalding said in an article in the *Catholic World* that one of the most pressing needs of the Church in America was the creation of a Catholic institution of higher learning. Spalding's astute sensitivity to American culture combined with his educational experiences in Europe, led him to believe that such an institution was absolutely necessary if the Church was going to effectively evangelize American culture and assume the intellectual status commensurate with its mission.

When the diocese of Peoria, Illinois, was erected, Spalding was appointed its ordinary. He was ordained a bishop on May 1, 1877. Not surprisingly, one of the new bishop's first priorities was Catholic education. He built schools and published numerous books and articles, especially on topics of education. He continued his campaign for a Catholic university in the United States and began to assume a national leadership role in Catholic education.

The new bishop of Peoria was a strong advocate of the Catholic school system and understood the focal point of education to be character training and intellectual openness, not merely subject learning and literary skills.[22] "Knowing and loving America, Spalding believed, then, that it was his duty to elevate his native land, to conquer for Christ the minds and hearts of his countrymen, and that this could be done only through education."[23]

Spalding's influence in the world of education reached beyond the Church as he became a recognized authority on the subject, even in secular circles. In his mind, all schools had to be institutions of moral formation, otherwise they had no claim to be centers of education. To this point, he once asserted at a House of Representatives subcommittee hearing before the Committee on Labor: "I contend that religion and morality are inseparable, and everybody who passes on questions of right and wrong is passing upon a question of religion as well as morality; there is no doubt of that in my mind."[24]

When the bishops of the United States gathered in 1884 for the Third Plenary Council of Baltimore, they also had Catholic education on their minds. They decided that a standard catechism had to be written for use throughout the country. Together with Msgr. DeConcilio, Spalding produced the final version of the Baltimore Catechism and guided it through publication. Practically speaking, Spalding was the primary author and editor. This catechism became the classic tool of Catholic religious education in the United States until the late 1960s.

Spalding was both a patriot and a loyal Roman Catholic. Like many Catholic thinkers in his day, he believed that the Catholic Church had "a great and beneficent mission to fulfill in an age and a country in which the individual has attained to the possession of the fullest liberty."[25] The Peoria bishop

> contended that the Church should, with dignity rather than in a combative spirit, enter into the living controversies of the age; should demonstrate that it was not opposed to culture and learning or the new developments in science; and that it should contribute to the literature and culture of the United States, and, in short, make its influence on American civilization felt. To do this, the Church must take into account the distinguishing characteristics of American life—its intensity, its initiative, its confidence in itself, its democracy, and above all, its faith in the future. It must re-direct these qualities from the lower plane on which they commonly flourished in America to the higher level of the spirit and of religion.[26]

Since his priestly ordination, Spalding had been of the mind that in order to fulfill its mission in the American Republic, the Church's greatest need was a distinguished Catholic university. He insisted that the grave weakness of American Catholicism was the lack of Catholic intellectuals who could respond to the challenges of the age, who could engage American culture on its own terms. The Church needed leaders who could "dialogue with modern patterns of thought and utilize the empirical sciences to respond to social and cultural problems."[27] Without an appropriate institution to cultivate this kind of leader, the Catholic Church's reply to American culture would always be inadequate.

Ultimately Spalding would play the leading role in the founding of the Catholic University of America. With his broad experience of the Catholic universities in Europe, and his own proven intellectual gifts and educational expertise, he was ideally suited to implant such an institution in American soil. He wrote to James Gibbons, archbishop of Baltimore, "If we could only begin a university college for the higher education of priests, it would be my greatest happiness to go into it and devote the rest of my life to this work, which, I am convinced, is of all others the most important and the most urgent."[28]

Despite an unfavorable response to the proposal from Cardinal McCloskey of New York, Spalding kept up the campaign. During a visit to Rome in 1883, Spalding solicited the support of Leo XIII and other Roman prelates, all of whom were in favor of the project. Returning home with renewed zeal, he delivered a sermon at the Third Plenary Council of Baltimore, explaining what the forfeit of a Catholic university would cost the Church in America. He said that "without this we shall vainly hope for such treatment of religious questions and their relations to the issues and needs of the day…without this in struggles for reform and contests for rights we shall lack the wisdom of best counsel and the courage which skillful leaders inspire."[29]

He concluded his appeal by emphasizing the American Catholic synthesis that would be the fruit of this beacon of education:

> Let there be then an American Catholic university, where our young men, in the atmosphere of faith and purity, of high thinking and plain living, shall become more intimately conscious of the truth of their religion and of the genius of their country, where they shall learn repose and dignity which belong to their ancient Catholic descent, and yet not lose the fire which flows in the blood of a new people; to which from every part of the land our eyes may turn for guidance and encouragement, seeking light and self-confidence from men in whom intellectual power is not separate from mere purpose; who look to God and his universe from bending knees of prayer.[30]

Cardinal Gibbons appointed a special committee in 1884 to study the matter; Spalding was a member of the committee. The Peoria bishop had secured a grant of $300,000 for the founding of the university from Gwendolen Caldwell, a young heiress known to the Spalding family in Kentucky. This, apparently, was the decisive factor. On December 2, 1884, the committee made its report in favor of establishing a Catholic university in a large and populous city of the United States like those in Dunboyne, Ireland, and Louvain, Belgium. Washington, DC, was chosen as the location.

After a letter of approbation from Leo XIII provided the necessary ecclesiastical authorization, the Catholic University of America was incorporated in the District of Columbia on April 17, 1887. On May 24, 1888, Spalding gave the address at the laying of the cornerstone of the first building at the new university, Caldwell Hall. President Grover Cleveland, several members of his cabinet, thirty bishops, and a large crowd of clergy and laity attended the ceremony.[31]

Cardinal Gibbons offered the rectorship of Catholic University to Spalding, but he refused, saying publicly that he was ill-equipped for the administrative post. Spalding continued to extend his energies and eloquence to the success of the university and was a member of the board of trustees until 1907. Gradually Spalding withdrew from the national scene and attended to the needs of Peoria. In 1905, he suffered a stroke, which limited his activities. He never fully regained his stamina after this misfortune and died quietly on August 25, 1916.

## The Work of John Lancaster Spalding Evaluated

Over a forty-year period, John Lancaster Spalding's sermons, lectures, essays, articles, and books made him the most significant Catholic educator of his time. One of the consistent themes in Spalding's concept of education was the paramount importance of Christian moral values and character formation. For him, this was the essence of education. He also promoted the cause of higher education for women, which challenged the established norm in his day. He was a strong advocate of liberty for scholars. Deprived of this freedom, he believed that Catholic intellectuals would be hampered in the quest for truth and in the ability to bring the treasures of

Catholicism to bear upon American culture. The Church had to encounter modern culture in order to exert its proper influence upon society.

Some of Spalding's opinions caused him to be associated with the Americanist ideas that were condemned by Leo XIII in *Testem Benevolentiae* (1899). At times, depending on the issue in question, Spalding did align himself with the leaders of the Americanist movement.[32] For example, "he ably defended the point of view that the Church must live in the present century, become a leader in criticism and in science, and within limits adapt itself to the spirit of the age."[33] Yet, "while he tactfully but courageously sympathized with the movement to adapt the Church to American conditions, his outspoken criticism of what he regarded as grave faults in our national life kept him from becoming an over ardent patriot."[34]

In many respects, during his tenure as bishop, Spalding "was an intellectual aristocrat whose independent mind and views differed widely from that of his more liberal confreres in the resolution of many of the basic issues that divided the American hierarchy."[35] He appreciated the pluralistic society of which he was a citizen, and at the same time was a defender of Catholic tradition. He realized that Catholics had to assimilate the culture in which they lived if they were to speak to it effectively. "But unlike Archbishop Ireland or Bishop Keane, his response to the crisis that beset the 'Church of the Immigrants' in the years following the Third Plenary Council of Baltimore was essentially conservative."[36]

What compelled Spalding was an idealist pursuit of truth that at times put him at odds with the established order. Above all, he wanted everyone to know that there was no conflict between being a loyal American and being a faithful Catholic. He was not blind to the defects of certain aspects of American secular culture, and liberalism in general, but he concluded that "the present state of Society is a fact which we cannot get rid of; consequently we must accept it and try to make the best of it."[37]

Throughout his ecclesiastical career, he attempted to develop a Catholic appreciation of the American pluralistic consensus. "Spalding recognized the essence of that consensus—a nation under God conceived in the natural-law tradition, a government by the people, and a free people who understood that freedom was not the power of doing what one likes, but the right of being able to do what one ought."[38] He appears to have had success in achieving a sincere and intellectually valid rapprochement between Catholicism and American ideals.

The crowning achievement of his attempts to fuse the gospel and American culture into a new Catholic synthesis in the field of education was the founding of the Catholic University of America. For him, education was the essence of evangelization in the modern world. Paying close attention to the cultural milieu in which he was immersed, that is, the American educational domain, Spalding strove to bridge the gap between Catholicism and American national values with zeal, balance, and perseverance. In many respects, Spalding's life and work present an excellent example of the Areopagus model of evangelization.

## The Areopagus Model Today

John Paul II noted on many occasions throughout his papacy that it is particularly difficult to transmit Christ's message in today's society, submerged as it is in a materialistic cultural ambience devoid of any inner dimension. This is especially true in the United States. In just a few generations, a major portion of the Christian denominations of America have devolved into large groups of baptized persons who have lost the sense of an authentic living faith, or have departed from the Christian fold altogether. The adherents of non-Christian religions amount to a mere fraction of the national population (less than 5 percent) as compared with the masses of fallen-away Christians.

As the unchurched default into secular materialism, they become conspirators in the dismantling of that which is historically most noble in the American tradition, its Christian culture. "Without doubt, it must be said that in no other period of history [was there such] a rupture in the…transmission of moral and religious values between generations."[39] This spiritual degeneration is at the heart of the moral malaise plaguing American society. A critical aspect of evangelization is to shepherd this corroded Christian culture of America back to its gospel roots.

In emphasizing the need to renew the societal fabric of our nation, we do not intend to reduce all of American culture to the consumerism, hedonism, violence, and selfish individualism that seems to prevail today. The United States has its virtues as well. It is still universally recognized as one of the most open, free, just, prosperous, and generous societies on Earth. In times of crisis the world turns to America, and we rarely fail to send aid to the needy or intervene on behalf of the oppressed. At the same time, our country is in great need of spiritual and moral healing. What is to be done? How is American culture to be re-evangelized?

To answer this question we must ascertain which factors most powerfully influence American culture, and consequently are dictating and monopolizing the social ethos of the nation. John Paul II identifies these factors as the fields of science and learning, education and entertainment, media and art, literature and philosophy, all "the worlds where the intellectual elite are formed."[40] It is these centers of influence that are redefining the country's cultural contours and are aggressively secularizing the distinctively Christian institutions and social standards of America.

The conversion of these "modern Areopagi" is an immense undertaking. Catholic historian Christopher Dawson gives us a point of departure in this task. He proposes responding to these secularizing power centers with a modern version of the Areopagus model of evangelization that is at once practical and inspiring.

First, as a preliminary caution, he advises today's evangelists not to attempt to compete with these dominant formators of mass culture on their own ground. If the Church does so, it runs the risk of becoming commercialized and politicized and thus compromising its unique values. On the contrary, Christians should accept their minority position and look for quality rather than quantity. "So it was in the days of primitive Christianity and so it has been ever since."[41] The Christian minority has the capacity to influence the majority, just like the secular elites, who themselves are a minority.

With this preliminary note in mind, Dawson proceeds to assert that the way to respond effectively to the modern Areopagi of American culture is to increase the intellectual significance of Christianity. The Church must confront secularism in the realm of ideas, for the intellectual factor has become the decisive one in our day.

In this engagement, Dawson does not propose a head-on philosophical confrontation. Instead, he recommends a program of intellectual formation *for the faithful* that is comprehensive and of the highest caliber. "The only remedy is religious education in the widest sense of the word. That is to say, a general introduction to the world of religious truth and higher forms of spiritual reality."[42]

Through education, believing Christians have "first, to recover their own cultural inheritance, and secondly, to communicate it to a sub-religious or neo-pagan world."[43] Dawson maintains that the net effect of this education would be an increase in the influence of Christianity and its values. In this emphasis on education, his thoughts are strikingly similar to Spalding's.

Dawson proposes a precise curriculum for this program of religious formation: the study of Christian culture. What he envisions here is not merely the study of Christian classics and literature, but an integrated examination of the sociological and historical sense of Christianity; its social and moral institutions and achievements. In other words, he advocates an appreciation of "how the Catholic Church built Western civilization," to coin Thomas Woods's phrase:[44]

> What we need is not an encyclopaedic knowledge of all the products of Christian culture, but a study of the culture-process itself from its spiritual and theological roots, through its organic historical growth to its cultural fruits. It is this organic relation between theology, history and culture which provides the integrative principle in Catholic…education.[45]

This course of study empowers the student to behold the "unity of Christian culture which is the historic basis of our civilization."[46] In this way she or he can grasp the basis upon which American society is built:

> What is vital is to recover the moral and spiritual foundations on which the lives of both the individual and the culture depend: to bring home to the average man that religion is not a pious fiction which has nothing to do with the facts of life, but that it is concerned with realities, that it is in fact the pathway to reality and the law of life.[47]

Ultimately the study of Christian culture leads the student to appreciate the truth that "there is an eternal reality beyond the flux of temporal and natural things which is at once the ground of being and the basis of rationality."[48] It enables her or him to realize that there is a moral and meta-physical foundation of history, and this foundation is most fully revealed to us in the New Testament.

The purpose of this study would be to provide ordinary Catholic students, who will eventually take up professions in the world, with a sense of the intellectual and spiritual riches to which they are the heirs. It would anchor them in the religious realities of life. It would equip them with the basic perspective and facility to engage secular society in a fruitful dialogue with Christianity. In other words, the study of Christian culture firmly roots believers in their own cultural and intellectual heritage. This formation enables them to encounter the culture of their age with confidence and vigor.

The study of Christian culture is also intended to prepare and motivate them to take part in the nation's ideological contests, and build a bridge of understanding out into the public square and interpret the Christian faith to the world outside the Church.[49] In this way the educated Christian becomes an instrument of the Holy Spirit, who has the capacity to permeate every sector of society with the light of God's own beauty, truth, and goodness.

Dawson targeted the field of higher education for this project. He thought it offered the best opportunity because it could be implemented with relative ease and minimal expense, compared with lower levels of education. His call for the study of Christian culture in the 1960s never materialized in Catholic institutions of higher learning.

His vision may not have fallen completely into desuetude. A new phenomenon has evolved in the post–Vatican II era that appreciates his inspiration: it is called the Catholic cultural center. These centers are pro-liferating, especially in the developed nations. They vary in orientation (theological, ecumenical, educational), in theme (cultural trends, values, art, science, dialogue, education), as well as in activities.[50] Yet their common concern is the relationship between faith and culture.

These hubs of Christian intellectual vitality are refreshing and effective instruments for promoting Christian culture through study, dia-logue, research, publication, intellectual formation, conferences, artistic events, and socialization. "They draw attention to the cultural projects and achievements of Catholic artists, writers, scientists, philosophers, theologians, economists and journalists, and promote enthusiastic personal commitment to values enriched by faith in Christ."[51] Following Spalding and Dawson, the Catholic cultural centers see education as the marrow of evangelization.

Perhaps these centers will become the new loci for advancing the intellectual merit of Christianity and for promoting Christian culture, which in turn may contribute to a spiritual revival in America. "If [American] society were once again to become [vibrantly] Christian, after a generation or two or after ten or twenty generations, this sacred tradition would once more flow out into the world and fertilize the culture of societies yet unborn."[52] This movement toward Christian culture would be marked, on the one hand, by wholly new expressions of the one true faith. On the other hand, it would presage "a return to our own fatherland—to the sacred tradition of the Christian past which flows underneath the streets and cinemas and skyscrapers of the new Babylon as the tradition of the patriarchs and prophets flowed beneath the palaces and amphitheaters of Imperial Rome."[53]

This hope may not be as illusory as it first appears, given the spiritual hunger so evident in contemporary American society.

## Considerations for Christian Education

There is a growing respect for the role of culture in the catechetical process today.[54] Religious educators realize that they must incorporate the concept of inculturation into the work of catechesis if their efforts are to be effective. In the United States, for example, the catechist working at the parish level cannot avoid encountering the culture of youth in the ministry of teaching. If the religious educator of the young does not acknowledge and in some way dialogue with this youth culture, the very message he or she is attempting to communicate to young people may be rendered irrelevant. This would be true in the education of everyone whose human experience is radically shaped by a distinct cultural milieu.

In many respects, Christian educators have to accept the "dialogue partners" that a given culture or segment of culture proposes in order to sow the seeds of faith within it. Of course, as catechists attempt to assimilate these elements into the mystery of Christ, this cannot have the effect of compromising or diluting the integrity of the faith.

The challenge for religious educators becomes one of appropriating the positive aspects of a culture in the service of Christian education, and setting aside those elements that propose a vision of life that is contrary to the gospel. In the ministry of religious education, there are moments when every catechist has to offer a prophetic witness to Christ. This is an ancient challenge that entails a dialogue with, and a purification of, the extant culture.

Discerning the parameters of proper inculturation is difficult; the Church offers catechists some guidelines for this process:

1. to know in depth the culture of persons and the extent of its penetration into their lives

2. to recognize a cultural dimension in the gospel itself, while affirming, on the one hand, that this does not spring from some human cultural *humus,* and recognizing, on the other, that the gospel cannot be isolated from the cultures in which it was initially inserted and in which it has found expression through the centuries

3. to proclaim the profound change, the conversion, which the gospel, as a "transforming and regenerating" force, works in culture

4. to witness to the transcendence and the nonexhaustion of the gospel with regard to culture, while at the same time discerning those seeds of the gospel that may be present in culture

5. to promote a new expression of the gospel in accordance with evangelized culture, looking to a language of the faith, which is the common patrimony of the faithful and thus a fundamental element of communion

6. to maintain integrally the content of the faith and ensure that the doctrinal formulations of tradition are explained and illustrated, while taking into account the cultural and historical circumstances of those being instructed, and to avoid defacing or falsifying the contents[55]

Catechists learn by experience that they cannot simply depend on a few experts to develop the methods of inculturation for them. Each catechist must necessarily be involved in the creative process of inculturation precisely where his or her community flourishes and ministry occurs. This inculturation has to "be an expression of the [catechist's] community itself and not be exclusively the result of erudite research."[56]

Good catechists possess the ability to inculturate the faith in the teaching process. They do this almost instinctively, although in some cases it may not even be done consciously. They are attentive to the cultural world of their students, reach out to them where they are, and attempt to translate the faith in terms familiar to them. Consequently, in their own way, their religious education classrooms become miniature cells of the Areopagus model of evangelization.[57]

CHAPTER VI

# THE LOAVES AND FISHES MODEL

## Charity

*Jesus healing and feeding the multitudes is the paradigm of the
Loaves and Fishes model (Mt 15:29–38). Experience shows that
the corporal and spiritual works of mercy performed by Christians
in the name of Christ are evangelizing actions that not only communicate the love of Jesus to needy people, but also inspire others
to turn to the Lord of mercy and compassion.*

### The Loaves and Fishes Model Defined

The public life of Jesus abounds with miracles that restored people
to physical and spiritual well-being. The Gospels tell us he healed the
multitudes, and *he had cured many and, as a result, those who had diseases were
pressing upon him to touch him* (Mk 3:10). Every time healing power went
forth from him, bystanders were at first stunned, and then moved to cry
out to God with praise and gratitude.

These spectacular events were moments when the power of Christ's
divinity shined through his humanity in dramatic displays of love. Jesus'
miracles were life-changing acts of mercy for those who received them.
They also caused everyone affected by them to turn to the Father: the
recipient's family, friends, and acquaintances as well as spectators and all
who heard the reports of the cures. These wonders were signs of the kingdom of God, the kingdom of love and peace, mercy and justice. As Jesus

said to his critics, *if it is by the finger of God that (I) drive out demons, then the kingdom of God has come upon you* (Lk 11:20).

These acts of surpassing love that Jesus performed while on Earth are a paradigm of evangelization. They compelled people to fix their eyes on the spellbinding recovery of the sick, the liberation of the possessed, the feeding of the hungry, then upward to the God who lay behind these manifestations of divine goodness. These miracles shook people out of their complacency, disposed them to listen to the Messiah, and demanded a response of faith. In Matthew's Gospel we read a typical account of the impact of Christ's healing love and compassion:

> *Moving on from there Jesus walked by the Sea of Galilee, went up on the mountain, and sat down there. Great crowds came to him, having with them the lame, the blind, the deformed, the mute, and many others. They placed them at his feet, and he cured them. The crowds were amazed when they saw the mute speaking, the deformed made whole, the lame walking, and the blind able to see, and they glorified the God of Israel.* (Mt 15:29–31)

Fundamentally, this narrative reveals the mercy of God, and how he uses his power to care for people in need.[1] "In this passage, we see fully displayed the graciousness and the sheer kindness of Jesus Christ. We see him relieving every kind of human need."[2]

The second sequence of this passage continues the divine movement of mercy (Mt 15:32–38). It tells us that after many hours, perhaps even days, of laying hands upon the sick, our Lord was moved to further pity by the hunger and fatigue of the multitude before him. Dismissing the objections of his disciples, he multiplied seven loaves and a few fish into more than enough food to satisfy over four thousand people. Here we behold the incarnate God revealing his true nature:

1. We see him curing physical *disability*. The lame, the maimed, the blind, and the dumb are laid at his feet and cured. Jesus is infinitely concerned with the bodily pain of the world; and those who bring men and women health and healing are carrying on the work of Jesus Christ.

2. We see him concerned for the *tired*. The people are tired, and he wants to strengthen their feet for a long, hard road. Jesus is infinitely concerned for the world's travelers, for the world's toilers, for those whose eyes are weary and whose hands are tired.

3. We see him feeding the *hungry*. We see him giving all he has to relieve physical hunger and physical need. Jesus is infinitely concerned for our bodies, just as he is for our souls.[3]

The New Testament reports that these works drew many people to Jesus. In fact, he may have converted more through these prodigies of love than through his preaching. The ultimate purpose of Christ's supernatural interventions was to promote the real goal of his mission, the salvation of all. As Leo the Great observed: "For as human ignorance is slow in believing what it does not see, and in hoping for what it does not know, those who were to be instructed in the divine lore, needed to be aroused by bodily benefits and visible miracles: so that they might have no doubt as to the wholesomeness of His teaching when they actually experienced His benignant power."[4] In other words, these acts of mercy inclined people to receive the saving grace of God through Jesus his Son.

Rudolf Schnackenburg commented on this passage describing Jesus' miracles and others like it throughout the New Testament. He made the same observation as Leo the Great: "it was precisely Jesus' efficacy among the people of God that is being brought out," and the fulfillment of the Messianic promises that is being confirmed.[5] As the crowds *glorified the God of Israel* (Mt 15:31) at the sight of the cures, "Jesus is once more delineated as the merciful Savior of the people."[6]

Jesus never wanted these signs to be understood merely as moments of physical, sociological, political, or economic liberation. Jesus' miracles were only a foreshadowing of the promise of eternity. After all, every person cured by our Lord inevitably suffered the ultimate fate of all human beings, the end of their earthly life. As he said after the miracle of the multiplication of the loaves and fishes, *do not work for food that perishes but for the food that endures for eternal life, which the Son of Man will give you* (Jn 6:27).[7]

Jesus exhorted his followers to imitate his acts of mercy and so lead others to the Father just as he had done. After proclaiming the Beatitudes, he told his disciples: *Just so, your light must shine before others, that they may see*

*your good deeds and glorify your heavenly Father* (Mt 5:16). Our Lord wanted
his followers to love as he loved—to cure the sick, feed the hungry, clothe
the naked, console the sorrowing. *Amen, I say to you, whatever you did for one
of these least brothers of mine, you did for me* (Mt 25:40).

As the early Christians fulfilled our Lord's command, these cumulative gestures of charity became a powerful sermon that caused even their
enemies to take notice. For example, the pagan writer Lucian (130–200)
admitted that "the earnestness with which the people of this religion
[Christianity] help one another in their needs is incredible. They spare
themselves nothing for this end. Their first lawgiver put it in their heads
that they were all brethren."[8]

When Emperor Julian (332–363) attempted to revivify the pagan
religion of Rome, he saw that one of the major impediments was the charitable work of Christians drawing many to Christ. Julian complained that
"Atheism [the Christian faith] has been specially advanced through the loving
service rendered to strangers, and through their care for the burial of the
dead. It is a scandal that...the godless Galilaeans care not only for their
own poor but for ours as well; while those who belong to us look in vain for
help that we should render them."[9] The fourth-century Church historian
Eusebius reported that these works of mercy inspired many pagans to
make inquiries about the new religion whose members displayed such
disinterested kindness to others.[10]

As the centuries progressed, "the Church spread further afield,
[and] the exercise of charity became established as one of her essential
activities...Love for widows and orphans, prisoners, and the sick and
needy of every kind, is as essential to her as the ministry of the sacraments, and preaching of the Gospel."[11] Many of these acts of charity
became institutionalized. The early Christian monks provided hospitality,
refuge, and works of relief for the sick and the poor in the vicinity of their
monasteries. Eventually this charitable activity on behalf of the poor and
suffering became incorporated into the mission of every diocese.[12] Orders
of religious and groups of laypersons also arose to care for the poverty-
stricken, the afflicted, and the victims of plagues.

The first public hospitals, like those we know today, were the creations
of monks, nuns, and devout laypersons. Then, in the Middle Ages the
Knights of St. John (later the Knights of Malta) advanced the concept of

the hospital for sick people with their institution in Jerusalem, where they treated not only Christians but Jews and Muslims as well.[13] Hospitals, orphanages, hostels, leprosariums, asylums, homes for the aged, shelters for wayfarers and the displaced, and a plethora of other similar institutions have their origins in Christian philanthropy.

All of these institutions communicate the light and mercy of Christ. This is the inspiration behind these works of charity. "In the history of the Church, how many other testimonies to charity could be quoted!...The figures of saints such as Francis of Assisi, Ignatius of Loyola, John of God, Camillus of Lellis, Vincent de Paul, Louise de Marillac, Giuseppe B. Cottolengo, John Bosco" are but a few lasting models of light within history.[14]

In our own day one of the most renowned personifications of Christian service is Blessed Mother Teresa of Calcutta's order of religious sisters, the Missionaries of Charity. Known around the world for their care of the poor, the Missionaries of Charity have been a quiet but visible force for evangelization. Their actions on behalf of humanity's most destitute have moved millions of people to consider the God who motivates the radical, self-giving faith behind this charity.

Mother Teresa's sisters understand themselves to be missionaries, evangelists, who carry God's love to others. They are "burning lights that give light to all men; the salt of the earth; souls consumed with one desire: Jesus."[15] Their stated purpose is evangelical, to work for the salvation and sanctification of souls by serving the poorest of the poor. Mother Teresa explains the missionary thrust of her foundation:

> We shall go freely in the name of Jesus, to towns and villages all over the world, even amid squalid and dangerous surround- ings, with Mary the Immaculate Mother of Jesus, seeking out the spiritually poorest of the poor with God's own tender affection and proclaiming to them the Good News of salva- tion and hope, singing with them His songs, bringing to them His love, peace, and joy. In spirit, to every part of the vast creation of God, from the furthest planet to the depths of the sea, from one abandoned convent chapel to another aban- doned church, from an abortion clinic in one city to a prison

cell in another, from the source of a river in one continent to a lonely mountain cave in another, and even into heaven and the gates of hell, praying with and for each of God's creation to save and sanctify each one for whom the blood of the Son of God has been shed.[16]

This they have done, and both the rich and the poor have been converted through their works of mercy. The self-giving goodness of Mother Teresa's sisters is merely one of countless expressions of charity offered by Christian communities and individuals around the globe. This way of presenting Christ to others may be called the Loaves and Fishes model of evangelization. In the American experience, the story of Rose Hawthorne Lathrop epitomizes this model of evangelization.

## Example: Rose Hawthorne Lathrop

In July 1851, Nathaniel Hawthorne wrote from his house in Lenox, Massachusetts, to a friend in Boston informing him of his new baby, a beautiful, healthy girl born on May 20 of that year. He hoped she would be the comfort of his declining years. Unfortunately, Rose Hawthorne was the joy of his life for little more than a decade. He died unexpectedly in the spring of 1864, and was laid to rest on the day before Rose's thirteenth birthday.

Although Rose was blessed with the companionship of her father for only a short time, there were many moments where his influence would have a remarkable bearing on her future. For example, Rose wrote many years later that her attitude toward the marginalized was profoundly shaped by Nathaniel: "The first influence came from that attitude of my father's mind toward both moral and physical deformity and corruption, manifested particularly in his writings where he shows clearly that he is a 'brother' to the abject element in mankind."[17]

Nathaniel Hawthorne exhibited this attitude in a stunning act of compassion when he was the American consul at Liverpool, England, while Rose was as yet a young child. The famous American author visited an asylum for the poor in his capacity as a diplomat:

Passing through the children's ward he came upon the most pathetic object he had ever seen—a little child, whose face and eyes were almost covered with scurvy. Although there were several other gentlemen in the party, the child singled out Nathaniel for special attention, prowling about him like a pet kitten, rubbing against his legs, and pulling at his coattails. Getting no response, the child stood in front of him, and with a pitiful smile, stretched forth puny arms in a mute appeal to be taken up. Although shrinking inwardly, sensitive Nathaniel could not resist the plea, for it seemed to him, as he acknowledged later, that God had promised the child this favor, and he could not refuse it, and call himself a man. Picking up the tiny tot, he held it in his arms for some time, and caressed it as though he had been the father.[18]

After the death of her father, Rose matured into an attractive, talented woman who enjoyed the benefits of travel, education, and the socialite lifestyle. She was devout and fully embraced the Puritan Christianity and the spirit of compassion that flourished in the Hawthorne family.

At age eighteen, she met a young writer named George Lathrop, the son of a New York doctor. They married three years later on September 11, 1871, and took up residence in Cambridge, Massachusetts. They were immature and financially unstable. George was struggling to succeed as a writer, and Rose was headstrong and fastidious, but these difficulties seemed surmountable.

In November 1876, the Lathrops were blessed with a son, Francis. It was also around this time that George began to show signs of intemperance that would later diminish his health and disposition. George was soon plagued with serious professional troubles and debt. Rose experienced little emotional solace in the marriage, and her world revolved around Francis until tragedy struck. On February 6, 1881, her little boy succumbed to a rapidly progressing case of diphtheria. Sorrow, disillusionment, and an increasingly distasteful incompatibility with George now afflicted Rose.

After Francis died, George and Rose moved to New York and sought many diversions to ease the blow. George's drinking became more of a problem. As he apparently crossed the threshold of addiction, it placed a severe strain on the marriage.

As Rose's marital dissatisfaction continued, she heard that an old friend named Emma Lazarus had fallen sick and went to see her. She could scarcely believe that Emma was afflicted with cancer:

> For a long time [Emma] had not felt well, but had done nothing about it. Now she was too weak to rise, even to greet her old friend; and Rose was deeply grieved at the change in her. She was consoled, however, at the thought that Emma had every possible amelioration that money and her loved ones could provide. Perhaps she could even be cured. Subsequent visits dispelled that hope, and despite tender care and the best medical attention, she failed rapidly and died within a few months.[19]

Rose had visited her often and saw firsthand the ruthless nature of the disease, as she witnessed Emma's fate from close quarters.

As this experience touched her in the depths of her soul, another interior awakening was set in motion. One day George brought home a copy of Cardinal Gibbon's *The Faith of Our Fathers* and gave it to Rose. The Lathrops soon began accompanying friends to Catholic services. The couple investigated Catholicism more intensely. "Suddenly, without warning, we see the unaffiliated but not unreligious Lathrops, converting to Roman Catholicism with an energy that can only be described as astonishing."[20] On March 19, 1891, George and Rose were received into the Catholic Church by Paulist Fr. Alfred Young, at St. Paul the Apostle Church in New York City.

The intimate circumstances and processes of this decision are difficult to trace.[21] The couple offered little explanation to their friends, and left no detailed account of their motivation and conversion experience. Some have speculated as to their rationale, but these attempts have only amounted to conjecture.

The Lathrops' conversion raised new hope that their marital problems might be overcome; unfortunately this was not to be the case. Rose was very unhappy in the marriage, and in 1894 she made the decision to ask the bishop of Hartford to grant her a separation from George, who had grown dangerously violent.

To outside observers the failure of the Lathrops' marriage came as a shock. To those who knew them well, it came as no surprise. According to historian Theodore Maynard, "it was the irreconcilable incompatibility of both, rather than George's drinking, that seems to have wrecked this marriage."[22] George was crushed by Rose's departure. They did not see each other again until George lay on his deathbed in April 1898.

Now Rose was alone and stripped of everything. She had no definite plans for the future, but she was determined to devote herself to others. It was at this point in her life that Rose confided to a friend that she desired to pick up and love the unlovely children of society. Amid the recent events in her life, "a [mysterious] transformation had been effected that was as startling in its own way as her marriage to George. But this change of status was to be permanent."[23] Fr. Young, the priest who guided Rose into the Church, encouraged her to heed these inspirations to devote her life to works of mercy. God soon pointed the way for her.

Rose heard that a seamstress she once employed in New York had developed cancer and was sent off to Blackwell's Island, the city's last way station for the destitute and the incurably ill. She was horrified to discover that once sick people were diagnosed with an incurable disease, they were automatically discharged from New York City's hospitals, and many of them were exiled to this forsaken place. Rose went to the island looking for the woman, who in the meantime had died there. On Blackwell's Island Rose found her new calling. "A fire was then lighted in my heart," she said, "where it still burns. I set my whole being to endeavor to bring consolation to the cancerous poor."[24]

Having discovered her purpose for the remainder of her life, Rose vigorously applied herself to learning as much as possible about the care of cancer victims. She completed a course in the nursing and care of cancer patients, and then she began an extraordinary new life. "She had failed as an artist, and achieved only minimal success as a writer. Her marriage had faltered, her only child had died."[25] Now, at the age of forty-four, she ventured forth from the comforts of elite society into the slums of the East Side of New York.

In the heart of the poorest section of the city, Rose secured a tiny flat, which she used as a base from which to care for the sick poor in their own tenements. She accepted no payment from her patients. Some of her former

113

friends were shocked, some were inspired, some were in utter disbelief. None of the reactions disconcerted her; she was undeterred in her mission.

Rose quickly found her charges: typically she clothed and fed starving mothers and their families, changed the bandages of cancer victims twice a day, comforted tuberculosis patients, and brought food to dying children. "I used to receive the sick and sore-beset at 8 a.m.," wrote Rose, "then go out till 1 p.m. on sick calls; then more patients came to be 'dressed' and to get advice and at 5:30 p.m. I started out for my visits to dress wounds, etc., with my heavy basket of medicines and salves, etc., on my arm, and fortunate to be able to return by 9 p.m."[26] Some financial support came to her from people of means who used to know Rose, but the daughter of Nathaniel Hawthorne also had to beg from the rich for food, clothing, and medicine for her patients.

Hawthorne's work on the East Side was not only grisly and grueling, it was also treacherous:

> The faces of the men and women she saw so alarmed her that she feared she would be robbed or even murdered if she were to live alone among such people. But in spite of these hazards, and many more she might encounter, she was determined to go on. Moreover, she knew on Whom to rely for help. "It was a lonely and frightened season in my determination," she confessed, "but I always thrust the care upon our Lord, assuring Him that I knew my incapacity."[27]

Rose's charity work took a decisive turn when she took in her first cancer patient to nurse at home. Shortly thereafter, she was forced to acquire larger quarters to accommodate other unfortunates. The sick came to her in great numbers and several physicians donated medical services. One day, praying before the tabernacle in a nearby church, she entrusted her work to the Sacred Heart of Jesus. She resolved then and there never to accept remuneration from any of her patients.

To enlist the help of the public in this enterprise of mercy, Rose wrote notices and articles in newspapers about her work and listed the items she needed. Several generous women came to assist Rose, but they did not stay long; the work was too hard and disgusting. The strain began to exhaust and overwhelm Rose as well. She prayed for co-workers who would grasp her vision and, like her, make a lifetime commitment to the poor. One day in 1897, a young woman arrived at the tenement, and she stayed. Alice Huber was an art student in the city and a daughter of a doctor from Louisville, Kentucky. Alice became Rose's most trusted friend, co-worker, and eventual successor.

On April 19, 1898, George Lathrop died at Roosevelt Hospital in New York City. He had continued to drink, which precipitated his early death. Rose arrived after George had expired; she knelt beside his body and prayed intensely for her husband, which she had never ceased doing since they separated. The description of her husband's death that Rose wrote in her diary two days after he passed, suggests that her love and respect for George was undying.

A mysterious consolation after her husband's passing was one of many graces that made Rose aware of God's inspiration in her life as an apostle of mercy. From the beginning, Rose understood her work as a religious undertaking, "for she knew that no support outside of religion could be sufficient to sustain it."[28] Moreover, her work on behalf of her patients and the interior experiences of her Christian faith were so intertwined as to be inseparable:

> God, in Whose sight no action performed with love is insignificant, often revealed His approval to her; and once in a most singular manner, as the following passage from the diary indicates: "On the first night, at 12, when I got up to say a prayer to St. V. de Paul I felt great happiness; and on the second night, not waking till 4 a.m. and getting up, I joyfully prayed, and saw our Lord, as if upon the Crucifix, not upright, but before being removed from the Cross."[29]

Rose reported having a vision of the Lord on one other occasion as well.

After George's death, Rose expressed interest in adopting some style of religious attire. Her faith in God was the motivation and strength that inspired her work in the slums, and so it was fitting to acknowledge this in some visible way. Rose and Alice approached Archbishop Corrigan with their idea; he received them kindly and encouraged their work, although he suggested they wait before starting some form of religious life.

Their service to poor cancer victims expanded, and they had to find a new home for the growing community of patients. Rose bombarded the media with pleas for help, and was able to acquire a house on Cherry Street, into which they transferred their "guests" on May 1, 1899. With this move Rose and Alice called themselves the Servants of Relief for Incurable Cancer. The house was named St. Rose's Free Home for Incurable Cancer. A supporter of the work, Fr. Clement Thuente, OP, proposed that the two women become the Third Order of Dominicans.

On September 14, 1899, Rose Hawthorne Lathrop became Sister Mary Alphonsa and Alice Huber became Sister Mary Rose. Although they were not yet able to wear a habit, they strove to live a more disciplined life. They recited the Little Office of the Blessed Virgin Mary and devoted time to regular periods of prayer and meditation.[30]

In November 1900, Archbishop Corrigan recognized their stability and their rigorous "novitiate" and granted them permission to take the habit. Their charism was concretely expressed in three principles: never show disgust at the sight of those disfigured by cancer; never allow an incurable patient to become a guinea pig for medical science; never accept money for their work, not even money from the family or a former employer of a patient.

On December 8, 1899, Sister Alphonsa and Sister Rose professed their first vows. As the number of patients at St. Rose's Home increased, so did the number of those who wished to join the new sisters. The home was soon bursting with both patients and postulants, and new facilities were badly needed. The prayers of the sisters were answered when they acquired a monastery with nine acres of beautiful property in Westchester County, thirty miles from New York City. They named it Rosary Hill. St. Rose's Home in the city was maintained by Sister Rose, who transferred patients to the new location in Westchester as the situation required.

In August 1901, Sister Alphonsa launched a magazine publicizing the work of the sisters entitled *Christ's Poor*. This periodical increased the fame of the Servants of Relief for Incurable Cancer, and widened the circle of their benefactors. One of Mother Alphonsa's steady and generous supporters was

Mark Twain. The New York papers followed Mother Alphonsa's work and divine providence provided for the needs of the sick poor.

In 1912, the home on Cherry Street in New York was replaced by a much larger building on Jackson Street, along the East River. Mother Alphonsa's community would eventually establish homes in Philadelphia, Pennsylvania; Fall River, Massachusetts; Atlanta, Georgia; St. Paul, Minnesota; and Cleveland, Ohio. The care of the destitute sick was now firmly ensconced in the cities and in the minds of America. Today the Dominican Sisters of Hawthorne are also in the process of establishing a home for the cancerous poor in Kisumu, Kenya.

Shortly before her death, Mother Alphonsa wrote in a letter to the editor of the *New York Times* a comment that prefigured the far-reaching effects of her mission: "Our method in caring for the support of our invalids is tedious indeed, but it seems to have been beneficial in many ways. We have a host of generous spirited letters of donations that show friendship has been won for all the future for the cancerous poor, not only among New Yorkers, but beyond the City."[31]

In 1926, Mother Alphonsa's health began to give way under the strain of the work. She died in her sleep, a poor woman, on July 9 of that year, at the age of seventy-five.[32] It is often said that her extraordinary apostolate was born out of sorrow. In the moment of her greatest need, the Spirit of Christ invited Rose Hawthorn Lathrop to rise above her shattered life and answer a call to serve some of the most forsaken of human beings, the cancerous poor.

## The Apostolate of Rose Hawthorne Lathrop Evaluated

The work of Rose Hawthorne Lathrop and her sisters is one of the most inspiring imitations of Christ in American history. Because profound works of mercy cross every human boundary and rouse every person of good will, Rose received awards for outstanding service to humanity from Church authorities as well as non-ecclesiastical institutions.[33] Yet Rose herself never tired of announcing that the root of her charitable activity was Christ.

Mother Alphonsa touched with her own hands and heart some of the most repulsively diseased persons on Earth, and did so with an unflinching compassion that seems almost too daring to be true. "To convert publicly

117

to religion is not rare; to practice the works of charity is not rare; 'to declare I wanted to be *of* the poor as well as among them' is the beginning of heroism."[34] Rose did this and taught others to do the same.

The corporal works of mercy performed by Mother Alphonsa and her companions are reflective of the Messianic signs performed by Jesus in Palestine: feeding the hungry, giving drink to the thirsty, clothing the naked, sheltering the homeless, visiting the sick, and burying the dead. The recipients of the sisters' acts of mercy were and are cancer victims steeped in poverty who are too poor to pay for their funerals. The sisters literally bury the deceased residents of their homes after caring for, comforting, and consoling them throughout their illness.

Why did Rose Hawthorne single out this segment of the disenfranchised as the focus of her ministry? She said, "I wish to serve the cancerous poor because they are more avoided than any other class of sufferers; and I wish to go to them as a poor creature myself."[35]

Perhaps one will raise the question of Rose's failed marriage as a flaw in her witness of charity. Rose and her husband, George, were confirmed in 1891 by the archbishop Michael Corrigan, a leading conservative in the American Church at the time.[36] Corrigan was fully aware of Rose's personal history. As the ordinary of New York, he was the one who gave canonical approval to the Servants of Relief for Incurable Cancer. Today Rose Hawthorne is a servant of God whose cause is up for beatification. It is best to allow the Church to judge whether her life can be called one of heroic virtue.

For over a hundred years now Rose's congregation, the Hawthorne Dominicans, as they are known today, has continued to serve these homeless and hopeless sick and dying cancer patients, regardless of creed or color. Thousands of cancer patients have come to know the love of God through the sisters' kindness and ministrations.[37] Countless Americans have seen the face of Jesus revealed in this sacrificial love as well. The work of Mother Alphonsa and her community is a prime example of the power of the Loaves and Fishes model to radiate the incarnate mystery of God in Christ.

## The Loaves and Fishes Model Today

The Loaves and Fishes model emphasizes the evangelizing effects of the corporal and spiritual works of mercy, "the service that [Christians] carr[y] out in order to attend constantly to man's sufferings and his needs, including material needs."[38] For the Church, these acts of charity are not a kind of social welfare program that could equally be left to the state to conduct. They are of her essence, and constitute an indispensable means of communicating and mediating the love of Christ to the world.[39] Throughout history the charity of believers has been one of Christianity's most convincing apologetics, and therefore one of the most effective means of drawing others to Christ.

There is also a prophetic side to the Loaves and Fishes model. Authentic evangelization not only looks to reflect the merciful face of Christ to humankind by serving the sick, the poor, and the abandoned; it also seeks to cure the causes of these conditions. As Paul VI said, "It is impossible to accept that in evangelization one could or should ignore the importance of the problems so much discussed today, concerning justice, liberation, development and peace in the world."[40] The very nature of evangelization demands that the prophetic voice of the Church impact social realities and call the entire community to conversion and repentance.

Issues like the dignity of the human person, the sanctity of life, the inviolability of the marriage covenant, the primacy of the nuclear family, the value of children, the dignity and rights of workers, morality and economics, commutative and distributive justice, subsidiarity, political and social justice, and the question of peace desperately need the light of the gospel. As a culture attains a certain harmony with Christianity, this "must never make the Gospel lose its subversive range, its absolute novelty with regards to every culture. The Kingdom of God is not of this world and the Church, by introducing this Kingdom, knows that it often has to struggle against worldly tendencies and powers that manipulate cultures" in ways that degrade and exploit people.[41]

The Church must challenge both developed and underdeveloped societies with the liberating values of the Beatitudes, even if it takes generations to inculturate these values. Men and women need to be touched by the wisdom of the Sermon on the Mount, and the words of Christ equating himself with the least of his brothers.

The preaching and witness of the Church has testified to these principles for twenty centuries. "She has always had and always will have a preferential option for the poor, just like her master Jesus Christ, the poor being those who suffer hardship and injustice from whatever cause; they are, therefore, of all social classes, but mainly from those whose deprivation is social and economic. Such people are not to be seen as a proletariat, but as sons and daughters of God, all of whom must have access to a decent livelihood."[42]

This dimension of the gospel calls Christians to enrich and permeate society itself with these moral perspectives. It calls the Church to proclaim the entire deposit of faith given by the Lord, which includes her social doctrine. In this way the Church makes "the message of the freedom and redemption wrought in Christ, the Gospel of the Kingdom, present in human history."[43] Therefore, the announcement of "the Church's social doctrine is an integral part of her evangelizing ministry."[44]

The mission of declaring the gospel would be incomplete if it did not take into account the concrete, personal, and social life of every child of God.[45] John Paul II clearly understood this gospel mandate. In his last book, his parting testimony, he said of his twenty-six-and-a-half years of Petrine ministry, that "this vision [of the Church's social teaching] has informed the way I have conducted my ministry of evangelization in a world which for the most part has already heard the Gospel."[46]

The preferential option for the poor is often taken to be a political position or an ideological statement. This is not the case if it is motivated by, and faithful to, a correct understanding of the christological and soteriological doctrines of the Old and New Testaments upon which it is founded. The social teachings of the Catholic Church over the past century have reiterated the gospel call to imitate Jesus. Our Savior lived among the poor and was committed to the least important members of society, whose lives seem to count for nothing in the eyes of the powerful. This commitment to the least of Christ's brothers is not about class warfare or party politics but rather the challenge to fulfill Christ's command, to love as he loved, and to establish his kingdom on Earth.[47]

As we saw in chapter V, the inculturation of gospel values is a process. Cultures will not suffer Christian transformation overnight. In fact, given the fallen nature of the human person, the evangelization of culture is an endless cycle of struggle against sin, both personal and social. Ultimately, the total redemption of culture will coincide with the eschaton, when Jesus Christ appears *to gather into one the dispersed children of God* (Jn 11:52).

In the meantime, Christians are obliged to live and proclaim the Beatitudes with fervor.

In this endeavor, believers are reminded that the prophetic reform of society is essentially a work of Christian charity, which "is first of all the simple response to immediate needs and specific situations: feeding the hungry, clothing the naked, caring for and healing the sick, visiting those in prison, etc…We contribute to a better world only by personally doing good now, with full commitment and wherever we have the opportunity, independently of partisan strategies and programs."[48] Rose Hawthorne grasped this point, and expressed it in a 1901 article in her publication, *Christ's Poor*. In this essay she commented on the idea of attempting to eradicate poverty without that love which St. Paul calls the greatest of all virtues. She wrote,

> Well may a sensible Empress advise that there should be "the greatest possible decrease in the numbers of the poor, by the removal of the causes of poverty existing in the poor themselves." When this nice point has been settled, poverty will be hoary with age, and crowns will have comfortably changed places down a vast line of heads…If time made any alterations in so vital a matter as the best methods of charity, Christ would have told us so…He has not said a word to contradict His first teaching, simple, direct, unavoidable, leading to personal sacrifice and immediate holy love…the greatest of the virtues.[49]

The reformation of structures is important, but promoting the charity of Christ is the Church's immediate duty. Personal acts of mercy offer something that systematic social reform cannot, that is, the look of love that every human being craves. As Rose Hawthorne proves, this love is not simply meeting material needs, but also requires spiritual care and refreshment that heals and satisfies the deepest part of the person.

In considering the Loaves and Fishes model in this light, it becomes evident that people will be moved to contemplate Jesus Christ not because of temporal stratagems or ideologies aimed at improving the world. Rather, he comes into focus through concrete acts of Christian charity "making present here and now the love which man always needs."[50] While acknowledging that the central purpose of Christ-like charity is not to proselytize, it must nevertheless be admitted that "a pure and generous love is the best witness to God in whom we believe and by whom we are driven to love."[51]

## Considerations for Christian Education

In the realm of modern Christian education, there has been a growing appreciation for the importance of the social teachings of the Catholic Church. The mandating of Christian service projects in sacramental preparation courses is just one example. Yet a great deal more has yet to be accomplished before this teaching permeates the consciousness and ordinary life of Catholics in the United States.

The magisterium of the Church asserts that "the concern of catechesis must not fail 'to clarify properly realities such as man's...search for a society with greater solidarity and fraternity, the fight for justice and the building of peace.'"[52] The Church exhorts the faithful and the clergy to study the history, methodology, and texts of Catholic social doctrine.[53]

The teachings of the Church's social doctrine are aimed at evangelizing the temporal realities of human life, but ultimately, "it is not the Church's responsibility to make this teaching prevail in political life."[54] The Church announces the truth, forms consciences, and prophetically confronts darkness. Her doctrine must be translated into action in the temporal order by the laity. In other words, "The direct duty to work for a just ordering of society...is proper to the lay faithful."[55]

Christian teachers have the challenge of maintaining these distinctions in the education for justice. Benedict XVI shed light on this challenge for educators:

> The Church cannot and must not take upon herself the political battle to bring about the most just society possible. She cannot and must not replace the state. Yet at the same time she cannot and must not remain on the sidelines in the fight for justice. She has to play her part through rational argument and she has to reawaken the spiritual energy without which justice, which always demands sacrifice, cannot prevail and

prosper. A just society must be the achievement of politics, not of the Church. Yet the promotion of justice through efforts to bring about openness of mind and will to the demands of the common good is something which concerns the Church deeply.[56]

This is why the Church asks catechists to teach the faithful about their civic obligations with consistency and fervor. In this way, these moral values can become incorporated into the cultural, social, economic, and political spheres of life, in service of the common good.[57] Sound religious education teaches that the virtue of social justice is necessary in the life of every Catholic. This instruction also makes "it...clear that no economic, social or political project can replace that gift of self to another through which charity is expressed."[58]

The realm of education is the ideal forum for discussing questions such as hunger, poverty, and disease, the danger of riches, and the moral responsibilities of Christians toward their neighbors.[59] Here believers can delve into these issues and the values that undergird them. In this context they will be enlightened and motivated to make a personal response. Christian education that does not address these questions is woefully incomplete.

# CONCLUSION

This book argues that six dominant models of evangelization emerge in Christian history. They can be identified in seminal form with specific New Testament passages. The St. Stephen model shows the strength of Christian *witness* to lead others to Christ, and is based on the martyrdom of St. Stephen (Acts 7:54–60). The Jerusalem model describes the evangelizing power of the sacred *liturgy,* and is discerned in the first Christian liturgical celebrations in Jerusalem (Acts 2:42, 46a, 47). The Proclamation model points to the *preaching* of the Word, and has its origin in St. Peter's first sermon on the day of Pentecost (Acts 2:14–41). The Fraternity model highlights the role of the *small community* in the propagation of the faith, and is founded on Jesus' selection and commissioning of the twelve apostles (Mk 3:13–19). The Areopagus model involves the *inculturation* of Christianity in the fabric of society, and looks to St. Paul's address to the Athenians in the Areopagus as its prototype (Acts 17:16–34). The Loaves and Fishes model calls attention to the evangelizing effects of Christian *charity* reflected in the corporal and spiritual works of mercy performed by his followers, and is typified in Jesus' healing and feeding the multitudes (Mt 15:29–38).

Each of these models of evangelization is readily observed in every age of Church history. In the American context, the St. Stephen model is illustrated in the courageous Jesuit witness before the native peoples of North America. The Jerusalem model was extensively employed by Junipero Serra and his fellow Franciscans as a primary means of introducing the California Native Americans to the mystery of Christ. The Proclamation model is portrayed in the parish mission crusade that revived the immigrant Church in the nineteenth century. The Fraternity model is represented by the mission of Fr. Isaac Hecker and the Paulist Fathers, the first religious order of priests founded in America. The Areopagus model is evident in the life and work of the great educator John Lancaster Spalding. The Loaves and Fishes model is strikingly revealed in the story of Rose Hawthorne Lathrop and her co-workers.

There may be other models of evangelization discernable in the New Testament, and there are many examples of evangelization to be found in American Church history. I have made the case that the six models proposed in this study incorporate the main features of Christian evangelization and effectively describe this mission of the Church.

No single model exclusively describes evangelization. The models are complementary and have always interpenetrated and interacted with one another in the course of the Church's life. Parenthetically speaking, one recent development in Catholicism that illustrates the interactive nature of the models is the Rite of Christian Initiation of Adults (RCIA). In its sequential ordering of steps and rites, the RCIA employs witness, liturgy, catechesis, fraternity, and service in a contemporary missionary dynamic that can be easily adapted to local traditions. Thus it offers a comprehensive process of evangelization that draws features from all six of the models. Tens of thousands of Americans enter the Catholic Church each year through the RCIA.

Each of the six models proposed in this book gathers together under a particular theme certain aspects of the biblical and historical data the Church possesses regarding the work of evangelization. The general approaches to evangelization expressed in these models have endured over the centuries in one form or another and have had innumerable applications in the experience of the Church. They offer a valid and useful means of identifying, describing, and categorizing the differing faces of Christian mission. The models, along with their accompanying examples, provide a typology that enables one to access, at least in principle, the complex reality of propagating the gospel and also to apply this reality to new situations.

The attempt to qualify and comprehend the work of evangelization through the use of conceptual models "will never be perfect because the Church, as a mystery of grace, has properties not paralleled by anything knowable outside of faith."[1] Nevertheless these paradigms have great utility in helping us to reflect upon, appreciate, discuss, draw inspiration from, and initiate the work of spreading the gospel. They offer valuable theoretical and practical starting points for the work of evangelization in every age.

The study of these models has raised a number of issues that transcend the models themselves and touch upon every aspect of evangelization. One of the first issues that arises is the theological tension between respect for endemic cultures and full missionary proclamation. Aside from secularism, one of the most prominent features of the missionary field today is cultural diversity. This diversity is a reality that has to be engaged with discerning appreciation. When Catholic evangelists approach people of another culture, their attitude must first of all be one of respect. "Bishops, priests, men and women religious and lay people need to develop a sensitivity to this culture in order to protect and promote it in the light of Gospel values, above all when it is a minority culture. Such attention to culture can offer those who are in any way disadvantaged a way to faith and to a better quality of Christian life."[2]

At the same time, we must be careful not to absolutize culture. It is not a reality that is fixed for all times. Cultural identities are temporal and therefore subject to change, evolution, transformation, dissipation, and even extinction.[3]

The Church esteems those elements of any culture that express goodness, truth, and beauty. In fact, these elements are excellent vehicles for advancing the fullness of God's self-revelation to humanity. Missionaries attempt to communicate the message of Christ to other cultures by creating a harmonious blend of feelings, art, ritual, music, song, decoration, and idiomatic expressions comprehensible to the people. This blending of faith and culture occurs most especially in popular piety.[4] The aim should always be to preserve the transcendental values inherent in every individual people or nation. To the greatest extent, the Church has tried to live by this standard. "Historical experience shows that the proclamation of the Christian faith has not *stifled* but rather *integrated and exalted* the authentic human and cultural values proper to the genius of the countries where it has been preached."[5]

In the evangelization of non-Christian cultures, the Church sends missionaries not only to proclaim Christ, "but also to seek and meet other believers and people of good will. The Gospel spirit directs Christians to accept, respect, listen to and try to understand these people."[6] If they respond positively, "dialogue is born and possible forms of collaboration are studied together."[7] Divine revelation is not something extraneous to this inter-religious exchange. By its very nature "it responds to an inner expectation within cultures themselves."[8]

By definition, missionaries are imbued with Christian certitude. They believe that Jesus Christ is the final and complete revelation of the one true God. No other religion or culture can add to or surpass the salvific mystery of Christ. Yet missionary encounters with other cultures can help to enlighten Christians in particular aspects of this mystery. Inter-religious dialogue can offer mutual enrichment because it opens up new possibilities for Christians *to comprehend with all the holy ones what is the breadth and length and height and depth, and to know the love of Christ that surpasses knowledge* (Eph 3:18–19).

All missionary initiatives should be the antithesis of imperialist conquest. Jesus the Good Shepherd is the paradigm of Christian mission. He *did not come to be served but to serve and to give his life as a ransom for many* (Mk 10:45). *Though he was in the form of God, did not regard equality with God something to be grasped. Rather, he emptied himself, taking the form of a slave, coming in human likeness* (Phil 2:6–7). Likewise, his disciples must be humble, self-renouncing servants of the many. Understood in this way, the Christian claim to religious truth is not a despotic program of dominion, even if errors in this regard have occurred in the past.[9] Like Jesus, faithful missionaries seek to be servants of the truth by being servants of others.

The effect of authentic evangelization is to transform cultures, not destroy them. As Benedict XVI explains, if Jesus Christ is the incarnate truth of God who gives definitive meaning to all of human history, then "this truth is the place where everyone can be reconciled and nothing loses its own worth and dignity."[10] Certainly Christian missionaries "must understand and receive the religions in a much deeper way than [they have] until now. On the other hand, the religions, in order to live authentically, need to recognize their own adventistic character propelling them forward to Christ."[11]

Walter Cardinal Kasper summarizes the attitude that should prevail among Catholic missionaries today:

Through every dialogue I not only intend to impart something to somebody else, I also intend to impart what is most important and dearest to myself. I even wish the other one to share in it. Hence in a religious dialogue I intend to impart my belief to somebody else. Yet I can only do so by paying unconditional respect to his or her freedom. In a dialogue I do not want, and am not allowed, to impose anything on anybody against their will and conviction. It is the same with missionary activities.[12]

 Cardinal Kasper's words highlight the fact that Catholic missiology today regards dialogue and proclamation as complementary counterparts in advancing the plentitude of divine truth.[13]

John Paul II is an ideal example of a missionary who thoroughly grasped the dynamic of dialogue and proclamation. From his earliest days he was convinced of the truth of Christianity; it permeated everything he did. He was always candid and sincere about his beliefs. The depth of his conviction defined him sharply within the borders of Catholicism. But John Paul II was also certain that radical fidelity to Christ commits the Christian "to an intense conversation with non-believers and with believers of other theological and philosophical persuasions."[14] As he said in an address to a United Nations assembly in 1995, "as a Christian, my hope and trust are centered on Jesus Christ...[who] is for us God made man,...[but] faith in Christ does not impel us to intolerance. On the contrary, it obliges us to engage others in a respectful dialogue."[15]

Thus we see John Paul II encountering eighty thousand Muslim youth at a stadium in Casablanca, Morocco, on August 19, 1985. Morocco is officially an Islamic kingdom. John Paul II's address to the young Muslims, spoken in French, was a tactful overture of friendship that did not exclude direct references to Jesus. First, he identified himself as the leader of the Catholic world and a witness of Christ.

For my part, in the Catholic Church I bear the responsibility of the Successor of Peter, the Apostle chosen by Jesus to strengthen his brothers in the faith. Following the Popes who succeeded one another uninterruptedly in the passage of history, I am today the Bishop of Rome, called to be, among his brethren in the

world, the witness of the Christian faith and the guarantee of
the unity of all the members of the Church.[16]

Then the pope affirmed the common faith of Christians and Muslims in the
God of Abraham, and in the moral values that they share. He called for a
united front to promote harmony, justice, peace, freedom, and brotherly
fraternity across the globe.

Toward the end of his lengthy speech, John Paul II did not avoid the
most challenging dimension of inter-religious dialogue, giving testimony
to his faith in Christ. The pontiff did this with both sensitivity and honesty:

> Loyalty demands also that we should recognize and respect our
> differences. Obviously the most fundamental is the view that
> we hold on the person and work of Jesus of Nazareth. You know
> that, for Christians, Jesus causes them to enter into an intimate
> knowledge of the mystery of God and into a filial communion
> by his gifts, so that they recognize him and proclaim him Lord
> and Savior.
>
> Those are important differences, which we can accept with
> humility and respect, in mutual tolerance; this is a mystery
> about which, I am certain, God will one day enlighten us.[17]

The young Muslims listened to the pope's words with a demeanor that
some observers likened to reverence.

In a visit to New Delhi on November 6, 1999, for the promulgation of
the synodal exhortation *Ecclesia in Asia,* the pope was more direct. In a land
where Christians constitute a tiny minority of the population, he encouraged
missionaries to continue their work. He praised them even as radical Hindus
demanded an end to missionary activity and perpetrated violence against
believers. "I hail the many priests, religious women and men and lay faithful throughout Asia who spend their lives for Christ and the Gospel," said
John Paul II.[18]

The pope firmly denounced religious intolerance and defended the
Church's right to openly proclaim her faith. He exhorted the Church of
Asia to pour herself out in "the saving dialogue which reaches out to the fol-

lowers of other religions and to all men and women of good will. In this dialogue, the word which we must speak is *the word of the Cross of Jesus Christ.*"[19]

In a final example of John Paul II's nuanced application of the principles of dialogue and proclamation, we see him addressing Catholics in Kazakhstan in September 2001. The speech was delivered during a pastoral visit to this nation of Christians with a large population of Muslim adherents. In the capital city of Astana, at a public outdoor Mass in the Square of the Motherland, the pope began his homily with these words: *"For there is one God. There is also one mediator between God and the human race, Christ Jesus, himself human, who gave himself as ransom for all"* (1 Tim 2:5–6).[20]

John Paul II explained that he came to Kazakhstan as an apostle and witness to Christ. Then he developed the theme of the one mediator in light of God's desire for the salvation of every person, and Jesus' self-giving in love for this purpose. "This 'logic of love' is what [Jesus] holds out to us, asking us to live it above all through generosity to those in need. It is a logic which can bring together Christians and Muslims, and commit them to work together for the 'civilization of love.'"[21] The remainder of the homily was an exhortation to Christians to transform the world according to the mind of God through prayer and good works.

These citations are representative of John Paul II's encounters with non-Christians. In each of these encounters he understood himself to be a Christ-bearer to the entire world, fulfilling the Great Commission. John Paul II wanted every baptized Christian to be infused with the same missionary spirit. He tempered his words according to the audience he was addressing without ever compromising his fidelity and obligations to Christ. He also sought and welcomed honest responses from his listeners. John Paul II exquisitely integrated the use of both dialogue and proclamation according to the demands of the situation.

In the American context, John Paul II exhorted Catholics to follow this same missionary program. In *Ecclesia in America,* the blueprint for evangelizing our continent in the third millennium, the pope expressed concern about those who did not yet know the name of Jesus. He was solicitous about their destiny because he said that by this name alone could they be saved. "Unfortunately," lamented the pope, "the name of Jesus is unknown to a vast part of humanity and in many sectors of American society. It is enough to think of the indigenous peoples not yet Christianized or of the presence of non-Christian religions such as Islam, Buddhism or Hinduism, especially among immigrants from Asia."[22]

The pope insisted that the evangelization of these people is urgent. He wanted American Catholics to introduce them to Christ. But he wanted them to use the same tactful, sensitive, and nuanced synthesis of proclamation and dialogue that he himself exemplified in his many decades of evangelization.

A second issue that surfaced in the writing of this book parallels the inculturation question. It has to do with the latent tension between Catholic evangelization and the ecumenical priority. At times, these two apostolic objectives seem to conflict, and ultimately militate against each other, or at least create ambiguity with regard to the mission of evangelization.[23]

In the Petrine ministry of John Paul II, this tension was viewed as an impetus for unity. "The task of evangelization involves moving toward each other and moving together as Christians, and it must begin from within; evangelization and unity, evangelization and ecumenism are indissolubly linked with each other."[24] The two are linked because their ultimate objective is the same: total conversion of everyone to Christ.[25] Regrettably, the power to accomplish this goal is hampered by the unseemly divisions that exist among believers. In this respect, evangelization and the achievement of Christian unity are also inextricably bound together.

In the work of evangelization, then, Catholics have to be sensitive to ecumenical issues. They have the manifold task of announcing the message of Christ in all of its fullness to the entire human race, and the commitment to work for unity within the Christian world. This is a delicate assignment. It requires courage, charity, personal holiness, sound theological formation, an astute ecclesial aptitude, and the inspiration and guidance of the Holy Spirit.

It follows that Catholic evangelists should avoid every form of proselytism, that is, the practice of inducing people to change their religious affiliation by using unfair or unscrupulous methods. Catholic evangelists should never employ moral compulsion or psychological pressure upon perspective converts. Nor should they offer education, health care, or material and financial gifts as a means of coercing people to embrace

Catholicism. The use of political, social, or economic power as an instrument of evangelization is likewise unethical.

Catholics also have to refrain from making unjust or uncharitable criticisms of other believers, or from making unfair comparisons of theological views.[26] In addition to this, it is important to recall that the central thrust of Catholic evangelization is not to target other believing Christians as such, but to draw everyone to the fullness of God's transcendent self-disclosure.

Nevertheless, Catholics are free and in fact obligated to offer an explanation of their beliefs to members of other denominations. The attempt to show others the reasonableness of Catholic doctrine in the face of objections and to establish the credibility of the Catholic position is required by the demands of both authentic proclamation and authentic ecumenism.

The right nuance of proclamation and dialogue once again provides Catholics with the key for engaging those with divergent views. The judicious counterpoise of these two movements ensures a harmonious product of truth, charity, and good fraternal relations, in this case, in the ecumenical forum.

In the context of ecumenism, the activity of proclamation is more properly termed apologetics because other Christians have already heard the gospel and presumably embrace the fundamentals of the faith. Beyond question, apologetic exchanges have to be free from a spirit of contention and harshness. In this setting, apologetics is characterized more by amicable discourse than by exhortation. As the *Decree on Ecumenism* states, Catholics must make "every effort to avoid expressions, judgments, and actions which do not represent the condition of our separated brethren with truth and fairness and so make mutual relations between them more difficult."[27] The apologetics dimension of Catholic evangelization should always maintain this ecumenical tone. Vatican II insists that

> the manner and order in which Catholic belief is expressed should in no way become an obstacle to dialogue with our brethren. It is, of course, essential that the doctrine be clearly presented in its entirety. Nothing is so foreign to the spirit of ecumenism as a false irenicism which harms the purity of Catholic doctrine and obscures its genuine and certain meaning.

At the same time, Catholic belief must be explained more profoundly and precisely, in such a way and in such terms that our separated brethren can also really understand it.[28]

On the other hand, ecumenical resolve should not inhibit the overall missionary proclamation of the Catholic Church. As Cardinal Dulles asserts, a robust ecumenism goes very well with an assertive program of Catholic evangelization. We don't have to be embarrassed about our convictions. We are free, and we are also duty bound by the Lord, to announce the fullness of the gospel as we have received it. He exhorts Catholic evangelists to "go with all cylinders" in their mission on behalf of the Church.[29]

John Paul II again demonstrates the correct way to balance adherence to the Catholic faith and the promotion of the ecumenical mandate. In his day, no one was a greater apostle for unity than he, and no one was more loyal to his Catholic identity. For him there was no conflict in this dual commission. In fact, his fidelity to Catholicism was precisely the incentive behind his strenuous efforts to reconcile the Christian family.

Without a doubt, the issues of inculturation and ecumenism as they relate to evangelization are complex. Returning to the question of the six models of evangelization, an evaluation of each of them in the light of these two issues is beyond the scope of this book. A thorough treatment of these topics would require the attention of entire treatises.

Finally, it appears that the distinctions between the six proposed models innately petition for a "unified field theory," some unifying principle that consolidates them into coherent facets of a single mystery of the Christian experience. I would suggest that the integrating principle is to be found in the fundamental purpose of the incarnation. "That purpose is [to offer people] a supernatural and eternal sharing in God's life."[30] As Jesus said: *I came so that they might have life and have it more abundantly* (Jn 10:10). The fullness of this divine "life overflows from the bosom of the Divinity to reach and beatify beings drawn out of nothingness, by lifting them above nature."[31] This sacred grace is communicated and received through Jesus Christ, the Son of the living God, by every person who accepts him as Lord and Savior. Faith in Christ makes human beings sons and daughters of the Father. This is the message Peter attempted to deliver on Pentecost; this is the truth Stephen witnessed to unto blood at the city gates; this is the mys-

tery re-presented in time and space in the sacred liturgy; this is the radiat-
ing font of a small community of zealous Christians; this is the interior
reality that transforms cultures; this is the grace that is made manifest
through the charitable works of Jesus' disciples.

The desire to see all men and women share in the very life of God
and thereby enjoy everlasting happiness with him is the meaning and
purpose of evangelization. In this sense, we can say that the invitation to
participate in the divine life of God himself through Jesus Christ his Son is
the unified field theory of the missionary mandate. This is the singular profession of Christianity in the realm of religions, "that it claims to tell us the
truth about God, the world, and man and lays claim to being the *religio
vera,* the religion of truth."[32]

Furthermore, "the pillar and mainstay of [this] truth...subsists in
the Catholic Church, which is governed by the successor of Peter and by
the bishops in communion with him."[33] This new life in Christ offered to
humanity through the mediation of the Church has been the perennial
content of evangelization beginning with the words of Jesus himself. It is
the driving force behind every act of heralding the gospel, past, present,
and future.

Regardless of the model employed, the Catholic evangelist is driven
by a burning faith. This faith is vested in the person and pronouncements
of Jesus Christ, who, with eyes raised to heaven, declared: *Now this is eternal life, that they should know you, the only true God, and the one whom you sent,
Jesus Christ* (Jn 17:3). Were this not true, all Christian evangelization would
be in vain.

# NOTES

## Foreword

1. Nancy T. Ammerman, *Pillars of Faith* (Berkeley: University of California Press, 2005). See especially the tables on pp. 117 and 134.

2. John Henry Newman, *Apologia Pro Vita Sua,* ed. Ian Ker (London: Penguin, 1994), 157. Newman is quoting from a letter written by him at the time.

3. Rodney Stark, *The Rise of Christianity* (Princeton, NJ: Princeton University Press, 1996), 208.

## Introduction

1. *Evangelii Nuntiandi* (Boston: Daughters of St. Paul, 1976), no. 14.

2. Some of the models in Avery Cardinal Dulles's book *Models of the Church* (New York: Image Books, 2002) parallel these models of evangelization: the Jerusalem model bears resemblance to Dulles's Sacrament model; the Proclamation model to his Herald model; the Loaves and Fishes model to his Servant model. (See chapters IV, V, and VI of *Models of the Church*.) Of course, the New Testament models proposed in this book are different in concept, emphasis, and application.

3. Stephen Neill, *A History of Christian Missions* (New York: Penguin Books USA, 1990), 35.

4. *Dei Verbum,* no. 17, in *Vatican Council II: The Conciliar and Post-Conciliar Documents,* ed. Austin Flannery, OP (Collegeville, MN: Liturgical Press, 1980).

5. *Ad Gentes Divinitus,* no. 5, in *Vatican Council II.*

6. Neill, *A History of Christian Missions,* 52.

7. Paul VI, *Evangelii Nuntiandi,* no. 14.

8. *Ad Gentes Divinitus,* no. 7.

9. Ibid. (How the Person of Christ and his Church relate to other Christian denominations and other religions will be addressed later in this study.)

10. Ibid.

11. Paul VI, *Evangelii Nuntiandi,* no. 14.

12. *Gaudium et Spes,* no. 37, in *Vatican Council II.*

13. John Paul II, *Springtime of Evangelization: The Complete Texts of the Holy Father's 1998 Ad limina Addresses to the Bishops of the United States,* ed. Thomas D. Williams, LC (San Francisco: Ignatius Press, 1999), 55.

14. George H. Gallup and Wendy Plumb, *Scared: Growing Up In America* (Princeton, NJ: George H. Gallup International Institute, 1995), Introduction.

15. Ibid.

16. Ibid., 71.

17. Benedict XVI (Joseph Ratzinger), *A New Song for the Lord,* trans. Martha M. Matesich (New York: Crossroad Publishing Company, 1997), 26.

18. Ibid., 27.

19. John Paul II, *Crossing the Threshold of Hope,* ed. Vittorio Messori (New York: Alfred A. Knopf, 1994), 112.

20. Ibid.

21. *Gaudium et Spes,* no. 13.

22. Fulton J. Sheen, *Peace of Soul* (New York: McGraw-Hill Book Company, 1949), 201.

23. Ibid.

24. Paul VI, *Evangelii Nuntiandi,* no. 18.

25. Ibid.

26. Sheen, *Peace of Soul,* 195.

27. Paul VI, *Evangelii Nuntiandi,* no. 27.

28. *Catechism of the Catholic Church* (San Francisco: Ignatius Press, 1994), no. 1431.

29. Sheen, *Peace of Soul,* 214.

30. Paul VI, *Evangelii Nuntiandi,* no. 9.

31. Christopher Dawson, *The Historic Reality of Christian Culture* (New York: Harper and Brothers Publishers, 1960), 18.

32. Christopher Dawson, *Enquiries into Religion and Culture* (London: Sheed and Ward, 1934), 327.

33. John Paul II, "Ecclesia in America," *Origins* 28, no. 3 (February 4, 1999): 3.

34. Dulles, *Models of the Church,* 2.

35. Ibid., 15.

36. Ibid., 12.

# Chapter I

1. Joseph A. Fitzmyer, *The Acts of the Apostles,* The Anchor Bible, vol. 31 (New York: Doubleday, 1998), 356.

2. Luke Timothy Johnson, *The Acts of the Apostles,* Sacra Pagina Series, vol. 5, ed. Daniel J. Harrington, SJ (Collegeville, MN: Liturgical Press, 1992), 135, 138.

3. St. John Chrysostom, "Homily on Acts, 17," in *The Navarre Bible, The Acts of the Apostles: Text and Commentaries* (Dublin: Four Courts Press, 1992), 88.

4. Fitzmyer, *The Acts of the Apostles,* 356.

5. Marion L. Soards, *The Speeches in Acts: Their Content, Context and Concerns* (Louisville, KY: Westminster John Knox Press, 1994), 70.

6. Fitzmyer, *The Acts of the Apostles,* 384.

7. Ibid., 390.

8. Ibid., 389–90.

9. Benedict XVI, Angelus Address, Monday, December 26, 2005, *L'Osservatore Romano,* January 4, 2006, 13.

10. Neill, *A History of Christian Missions,* 38–39.

11. John Henry Cardinal Newman, *An Essay in Aid of a Grammar of Assent,* in *The Works of Cardinal Newman* (London: Longmans, Green, and Co., 1898), 478.

12. Ibid., 477–78.

13. *A Testimony by St. Chantal,* ed. Elizabeth Stopp (Hyattsville, MD: Institute of Salesian Studies, 1967), 127.

14. Ibid., 129.

15. Jordan Aumann, *Christian Spirituality in the Catholic Tradition* (San Francisco: Ignatius Press, 1986), 267.

16. Beatification of Three Servants of God: Sunday, November 13, 2005, *L'Osservatore Romano,* November 23, 2005, 5.

17. Jean-Jacques Antier, *Charles de Foucauld,* trans. Julia Shirek Smith (San Francisco: Ignatius Press, 1997), 264–65.

18. John Paul II, *Novo Millennio Ineunte* (Boston: St. Paul Books and Media, 2001), no. 27.

19. John Paul II, *Redemptoris Missio* (Boston: St. Paul Books and Media, 1991), no. 42.

20. Paul VI, *Evangelii Nuntiandi,* no. 21.

21. John Paul II, *Novo Millennio Ineunte,* no. 7.

22. Christopher Vecsey, *The Paths of Kateri's Kin* (Notre Dame, IN: University of Notre Dame Press, 1997), 10.

23. Patrick W. Carey, *Catholics in America: A History* (Westport, CT: Praeger Publishers, 2004), 8.

24. Jon Butler, Grant Wacker, and Randall Balmer, *Religion in American Life: A Short History* (New York: Oxford University Press, 2003), 43–44; John Gilmary Shea, *History of the Catholic Missions Among the Indian Tribes of the United States* (New York: P. J. Kenedy, 1881), 128.

25. James Hennesey, SJ, *American Catholics* (New York: Oxford University Press, 1983), 23.

26. John Tracey Ellis, *American Catholicism,* 2nd ed. (Chicago: University of Chicago Press, 1969), 12.

27. Hennesey, *American Catholics,* 25.

28. Theodore Maynard, *Great Catholics in American History* (Garden City, NY: Hanover House, 1957), 20.

29. Martin J. Scott, SJ, *Isaac Jogues: Missioner and Martyr* (New York: P. J. Kenedy and Sons, 1927), 85.

30. Madeline Grace, "Under Shadows of Death: The Spiritual Journey of Jean de Brebeuf and Isaac Jogues," *American Catholic Studies* 115, no. 3 (Fall 2004): 60.

31. Vecsey, *Kateri's Kin,* 99.

32. Carey, *Catholics in America,* 9.

33. Jay P. Dolan, *The American Catholic Experience* (Notre Dame, IN: University of Notre Dame Press, 1992), 22.

34. Shea, *Missions Among the Indians,* 25–26.

35. Carey, *Catholics in America,* 8.

36. Shea, *Mission Among the Indians,* 26.

37. Margaret R. Bunson, *Kateri Tekakwitha: Mystic of the Wilderness* (Huntington, IN: Our Sunday Visitor, 1992), 29.

38. Edwin Gaustad and Leigh Schmidt, *The Religious History of America* (San Francisco: HarperCollins Publishers, 2004), 11.

39. Vecsey, *Kateri's Kin,* 10–12.

40. Ibid., 25.

41. Dolan, *American Experience,* 41.

42. Carey, *Catholics in America,* 9.

43. Ibid.

44. Ibid.

45. Ibid., 10.

46. It must be admitted that not every Christian Native American today is enamored with the Jesuit effort to evangelize his or her ancestors. See Vecsey, *Kateri's Kin,* 101–8.

47. Diana L. Eck, *A New Religious America* (San Francisco: HarperCollins Publishers, 2001), 1.

48. For example, a study by the National Opinion Research Center in Chicago puts the total number of Muslims in the United States today at a modest figure of 2 million.

49. Richard J. Neuhaus, in his book *The Naked Public Square* (Grand Rapids, MI: Eerdmans Publishing Co., 1984), analyzes the exclusion of religious expression from American public life and argues convincingly why this is not only unjust and un-American, but ultimately gravely harmful to democracy.

50. Yale law professor Stephen L. Carter, in his book *The Culture of Disbelief: How American Law and Politics Trivialize Religious Devotion* (New York: Basic Books, 1993), effectively demonstrates how contemporary political structures trivialize the faith of millions in America, and that this endangers the vitality of our democratic system.

51. David Smith, *Mission After Christendom* (London: Darton, Longman and Todd, Ltd, 2003), 9.

52. Ibid., 123.

53. Eddie Gibbs, "Evangelization in the Catholic Church: An Evangelical Reflection," in *Evangelizing America,* ed. Thomas P. Rausch, SJ (Mahwah, NJ: Paulist Press, 2004), 131.

54. Benedict XVI, Angelus Address, Monday, December 26, 2005, *L'Osservatore Romano,* January 4, 2006, 13.

55. Smith, *Mission After Christendom,* 112.

56. *Evangelii Nuntiandi,* no. 41.

57. John Paul II, *Redemptoris Missio,* no. 23.

58. *Lumen Gentium,* no. 40, in *Vatican Council II.*

59. John Paul II, *Novo Millennio Ineunte,* no. 31.

60. In addition to *Lumen Gentium,* chapter 4, "The Call to Holiness," another excellent resource for the religious educator on this topic is *The Introduction to the Devout Life,* by St. Francis de Sales, trans. John K. Ryan (New York: Doubleday, 1989).

61. *Lumen Gentium,* no. 17.

62. Ibid., no. 35 (author's italics).

63. John Paul II, *Novo Millennio Ineunte,* no. 16.

# Chapter II

1. *The Navarre Bible, The Acts of the Apostles: Texts and Commentaries,* 52; Jacques Dupont, OSB, "The Meal at Emmaus," in *The Eucharist in the New Testament: A Symposium,* trans. M. E. Stewart (Baltimore: Helicon Press, 1965), 115–21; Rudolf Schnackenburg, *The Church in the New Testament,* trans. W. J. O'Hara (New York: Seabury Press, 1965), 40.

2. *The Teaching of the Twelve Apostles,* trans. M. B. Riddle, DD, in *Ante-Nicene Fathers,* vol. 7, ed. Alexander Roberts and James Donaldson (Peabody, MA: Hendrickson Publishers, 1995), 379–81.

3. Schnackenburg, *The Church in the New Testament,* 42.

4. Benedict XVI, *A New Song for the Lord,* 129.

5. Neill, *A History of Christian Missions,* 42.

6. Odo Casel, as quoted in Romano Guardini, *The Spirit of the Liturgy* (New York: Crossroad Publishing Company, 1998), 83.

7. Christopher Dawson, *Religion and the Rise of Western Culture* (New York: Sheed and Ward, 1950), 40.

8. Ibid., 40–41.

9. Christopher Dawson, *The Formation of Christendom* (New York: Sheed and Ward, 1967), 139.

10. Dawson, *The Historic Reality of Christian Culture,* 36.

11. John Paul II, "The Liturgy and Its Renewal," *Origins* 21, no. 4 (November 5, 1998).

12. Benedict XVI, *A New Song for the Lord,* 77.

13. Guardini, *The Spirit of the Liturgy,* 49.

14. Ibid., 24.

15. Frank C. Senn, *The Witness of the Worshiping Community* (Mahwah, NJ: Paulist Press, 1993), 30.

16. John Paul II, *Ad limina* Address to French Bishops, March 8, 1997, *L'Osservatore Romano,* March 19, 1997, 5.

17. St. Augustine, *The Confessions,* trans. J. G. Pilkington, in *Nicene and Post-Nicene Fathers,* vol. 1, ed. Philip Schaff (Peabody, MA: Hendrickson Publishers, 1995), 134.

18. Benedict XVI, *A New Song for the Lord,* 109–10.

19. *Sacrosanctum Concilium,* no. 10, in *Vatican Council II.*

20. Ibid., no. 2.

21. Ibid., no. 10.

22. Paul VI, *Evangelii Nuntiandi,* no. 47.

23. Benedict XVI, *A New Song for the Lord,* 175.

24. Dolan, *The American Catholic Experience,* 19.

25. *Documents of American Catholic History,* ed. John Tracy Ellis (Milwaukee: Bruce Publishing Company, 1956), 9.

26. Dolan, *The American Catholic Experience,* 25.

27. MNL Couvre De Murville, *The Man Who Founded California: The Life of Blessed Junipero Serra* (San Francisco: Ignatius Press, 2000), 43.

28. Shea, *Catholic Missions,* 116.

29. John Tracy Ellis, *Catholics in Colonial America* (Baltimore: Helicon Press, 1965), 116–17.

30. *Documents,* 45.

31. Christopher Vecsey, *On the Padres' Trail* (Notre Dame, IN: University of Notre Dame Press, 1996), 239.

32. De Murville, *The Man Who Founded California,* 38–39.

33. Vecsey, *On the Padres' Trail,* 240.

34. Ibid., 240–41.

35. De Murville, *The Man Who Founded California,* 38–39.

36. Vecsey, *On the Padres' Trail,* 239, 243.

37. De Murville, *The Man Who Founded California,* 69–71.

38. Ibid., 67–68.

39. Ibid., 114–16.

40. Ibid., 117.

41. Thomas Merton, "Conquistador, Tourist and Indian," in *Saints and Sinners,* ed. Greg Tobin (New York: Doubleday, 1999), 80.

42. Vecsey, *On the Padres' Trail,* 347–64, 379–93.

43. Dolan, *American Experience,* 24.

44. *Documents,* 8.

45. Ibid., 8–9.

46. Ellis, *Colonial America,* 56.

47. De Murville, *The Man Who Founded California,* 37.

48. Ibid., 92.

49. Ibid., 122.

50. Ibid., 102–3.

51. Congregation for the Evangelization of Peoples, *Guida delle Missioni Cattoliche* (Rome, 1989), 12. See Giuseppe Buono, *Missiology: Theology and Praxis* (Nairobi: Paulines Publications Africa, 2002), 138.

52. Buono, *Missiology,* 141.

53. Paul VI, *Evangelii Nuntiandi,* no. 65.

54. Ibid., no. 53.

55. Benedict XVI, Angelus Address, October 23, 2005, *L'Osservatore Romano,* October 26, 2005, 17.

56. *Sacrosanctum Concilium,* no. 9.

57. Thomas Dubay, *The Evidential Power of Beauty* (San Francisco: Ignatius Press, 1999), 339.

58. *Presbyterorum Ordinis,* no. 5, in *Vatican Council II.*

59. John Paul II, *Ecclesia de Eucharistia* (Boston: Pauline Books and Media, 2003), nos. 48–49.

60. Ibid., no. 48.

61. Bishop's Committee on the Liturgy, *Environment and Art in Catholic Worship* (Washington, DC: United States Catholic Conference, 1978), 21.

62. Hans Urs von Balthasar, "The Grandeur of the Liturgy," *Communio International Catholic Review* 5, no. 4 (Winter 1978): 349.

63. Ibid., 346–47.

64. Ibid., 344.

65. Ibid., 348.

66. *Eucharisticum Mysterium,* no. 12, in *Vatican Council II.*

67. Ibid., no. 3 g.

68. Aumann, *Christian Spirituality,* 267.

69. Malcolm M. Kennedy, "Evangelization and the Call to Holiness," in *The Church's Mission of Evangelization*, ed. William E. May (Steubenville, OH: Franciscan University Press, 1996), 207.

70. John Paul II, *Novo Millennio Ineunte,* no. 38.

71. *Catechism of the Catholic Church* (San Francisco: Ignatius Press, 1994), no. 1095.

72. *Sacrosanctum Concilium,* no. 14.

73. Ibid.

74. George Weigel, *The Truth of Catholicism* (New York: HarperCollins Publishers, 2001), 63–64.

75. John Paul II, *Redemptoris Hominis* (Washington, DC: United States Catholic Conference, 1979), no. 20.

76. *Catechism,* no. 1367.

77. Ibid., no. 1374.

78. Ibid., no. 1391.

79. John Paul II, "The Liturgy and Its Renewal," 379.

80. Ibid.

81. *Eucharisticum Mysterium,* no. 3 b, c.

82. John Paul II, "The Liturgy and Its Renewal," 379.

83. Ibid.

84. Resources on this topic that may be helpful to religious educators include two works by Benedict XVI, *A New Song for the Lord: Faith in Christ and Liturgy Today* (1997), trans. Martha M. Matesich, and *The Spirit of the Liturgy* (2000), trans. John Saward, both published by Ignatius Press in San Francisco.

85. Dawson, *The Historic Reality of Christian Culture,* 18.

# Chapter III

1. Eddie Gibbs, "The Launching of Mission: The Outpouring of the Spirit at Pentecost," in *Mission in Acts: Ancient Narratives in Contemporary Context,* ed. Robert L. Gallagher and Paul Hertzig (Maryknoll, NY: Orbis Books, 2004), 22.

2. Fitzmyer, *The Acts of the Apostles,* 248.

3. Gibbs, *Mission in Acts,* 22.

4. Fitzmyer, *The Acts of the Apostles,* 248.

5. Schnackenburg, *The Church in the New Testament,* 37–38.

6. John Paul II, *Redemptoris Missio,* no. 44.

7. John Paul II, *Ecclesia in America,* no. 66.

8. *Dei Verbum,* nos. 8, 9.

9. *Following Christ in Mission: A Foundation Course in Missiology*, ed. Sebastian Karotemprel (Nairobi: Pauling Publications Africa, 1995), 93–94.

10. John Paul II, *Redemptoris Missio,* no. 46.

11. *Following Christ in Mission,* 94.

12. *Dei Verbum,* no. 5.

13. Congregation for the Clergy, *General Directory For Catechesis* (Washington, DC: United States Catholic Conference, 1998), no. 62.

14. John Paul II, *Catechesi Tradendae* (Boston: Daughters of St. Paul, 1980), nos. 18, 20.

15. Ibid., no. 21.

16. Jay P. Dolan, *Catholic Revivalism: The American Experience 1830–1900* (Notre Dame: University of Notre Dame Press, 1978), xvi.

17. John A. Berger, CSSR, *Life of Right Rev. John N. Neumann, DD,* trans. Eugene Grimm (New York: Benzinger Brothers, 1884), 267.

18. Dolan, *Catholic Revivalism,* 11.

19. Berger, *Life of Neumann,* 257.

20. Dolan, *Catholic Revivalism,* 18.

21. Ibid., 19.

22. Joseph P. Chinnici, OFM, *Living Stones: The History and Structure of Catholic Spiritual Life in the United States* (Maryknoll, NY: Orbis Books, 1996), 64.

23. Dolan, *Catholic Revivalism,* 33.

24. Ibid., 84–85.

25. Michael J. Curley, CSSR, *Bishop John Neumann* (Philadelphia: Bishop Neumann Center, 1952), 160.

26. Dolan, *Catholic Revivalism,* 202.

27. Ibid., 191–92.

28. Chinnici, *Living Stones,* 72.

29. Dolan, *Catholic Revivalism,* 191.

30. Ibid., 181.

31. Ibid., 146–47.

32. Ibid.

33. Ibid., 196.

34. Curley, *Bishop Neumann,* 353.

35. *Lumen Gentium,* no. 1.

36. *Evangelii Nuntiandi,* no. 22.

37. Archbishop Sean O'Malley, "Why Preaching Must Be a Priority Today," *Origins* 33, no. 45 (April 22, 2004): 771.

38. Ibid., 773.

39. Ibid.

40. Ibid.

41. Thom S. Rainer, *Surprising Insights from the Unchurched: And Proven Ways to Reach Them* (Grand Rapids, MI: Zondervan, 2001).

42. Ibid., 21.

43. Ibid., 143–45.

44. O'Malley, "Why Preaching Must Be a Priority Today," 772.

45. Avery Cardinal Dulles, "The Rebirth of Apologetics," *First Things* 143 (May 2004): 23.

46. Colleen Carroll, *The New Faithful: Why Young Adults Are Embracing Christian Orthodoxy* (Chicago: Loyola Press, 2002), 18.

47. Ibid., 12.

48. Ibid., 9.

49. Ibid., 10.

50. *Dei Verbum,* nos. 7, 8, 9.

51. *Lumen Gentium,* no. 25.

52. *Donum Veritatis,* Congregation for the Doctrine of the Faith (1990), in *The Christian Faith in the Doctrinal Documents of the Catholic Church Series,* ed. Jacques Dupuis (New York: Alba House, 1995), 77–82.

53. Paul VI, *Evangelii Nuntiandi,* no. 53.

54. Rainer, *Surprising Insights from the Unchurched,* 67, 220.

55. *General Catholic Directory For Catechesis,* no. 35.

56. Bishop Donald Wuerl, "A Look Inside the New U.S. Catechetical Directory," *Origins* 34, no. 33 (February 3, 2005): 529.

57. John Paul II, *Juvenum Patris,* Acts of The General Council of the Salesian Society of St. John Bosco (New Rochelle, NY: Salesian Communications, 1988), nos. 16, 30.

58. To learn about the pedagogy of holiness as a philosophy of education, see *The Educational Philosophy of St. John Bosco* by John Morrison (New Rochelle, NY: Salesiana Publications, 1979) or *Keys to the Hearts of Youth: St. John Bosco's Pastoral and Educational Mission, A Spirituality and Methodology* by Paul P. Avallone, SDB (New Rochelle, NY: Salesiana Publications, 1999).

59. Edward F. Garesche, *The Everyday Apostle: Commonsense Ways to Draw Others to Christ* (Manchester: NH: Sophia Institute Press, 2002), 19–24.

60. *Inter Mirifica,* nos. 13, 17, in *Vatican Council II.*

# Chapter IV

1. William Barclay, *The Gospel of Mark* (Louisville, KY: John Knox Press, 2001), 83.

2. Benedict XVI (Joseph Ratzinger), *Called to Communion,* trans. Adrian Walker (San Francisco: Ignatius Press, 1996), 25.

3. John R. Donahue and Daniel J. Harrington, SJ, *The Gospel of Mark,* Sacra Pagina Series, vol. 2, ed. Daniel J. Harrington, SJ (Collegeville, MN: Liturgical Press, 2002), 123, 127.

4. Benedict XVI, *Called to Communion,* 25.

5. Ezra P. Gould, *The Critical and Exegetical Commentary on the Gospel According to Saint Mark* (Edinburgh: T & T Clark, 1996), 59.

6. The overall success of this effort must take into account the ministry of St. Paul, an apostle *born out of the normal course* (1 Cor 15:8), and other leaders named in the New Testament, plus the many nameless associates who joined in the work of announcing the gospel. In those days every new convert became another zealous evangelist of "the way."

7. Benedict XVI, *Without Roots,* trans. Michael F. Moore (New York: Basic Books, 2006), 120–23.

8. Dom Jean-Baptiste Chautard, OCSO, *The Soul of the Apostolate,* trans. Monk of Our Lady of Gethsemani (Trappist, KY: Abbey of Gethsemani, 1946), 162.

9. Ibid., 165.

10. *Apostolicam Actoustitem,* no. 2, in *Vatican Council II.*

11. Chautard, *The Soul of the Apostolate,* 167–68.

12. Ibid., 172.

13. Paul Turks, *Philip Neri: The Fire of Joy,* trans. Daniel Utrecht (Staten Island, NY: Alba House, 1995), 41–48.

14. David J. O'Brien, *Isaac Hecker: An American Catholic* (Mahwah, NJ: Paulist Press, 1992), 17.

15. Vincent F. Holden, CSP, *The Yankee Paul: Isaac Thomas Hecker* (Milwaukee: Bruce Publishing Company, 1958), 25.

16. Ibid., 95.

17. O'Brien, *An American Catholic,* 89.

18. Ibid., 87.

19. Ibid., 90.

20. Paul Robichaud, CSP, "Evangelizing America: Transformations in Paulist Mission," *US Catholic Historian* 2, no. 2 (Spring 1993): 63–64.

21. Ibid., 64.

22. Ibid., 62.

23. O'Brien, *An American Catholic,* 186.

24. Ibid., 208.

25. Ibid., 206.

26. *The Encyclopedia of American Catholic History,* ed. Michael Glazier and Thomas J. Shelley (Collegeville, MN: Liturgical Press, 1997), 625.

27. Ibid., 1119.

28. Robichaud, "Evangelizing America," 67.

29. Ibid.

30. Ibid., 70–72.

31. Ibid., 74.

32. Ibid., 74–78.

33. *Documents,* 350.

34. Robichaud, "Evangelizing America," 78.

35. Benedict XVI, Christmas, The Council and Conversion in Christ, *L'Osservatore Romano,* January 4, 2006, 5.

36. Ibid.

37. Ibid.

38. Ibid.

39. Ibid.

40. Ibid.

41. Ibid., 6.

42. Ibid.

43. O'Brien, *An American Catholic,* 90.

44. Paul VI, *Evangelii Nuntiandi,* no. 77.

45. John Paul II, *Ut Unum Sint* (Washington, DC: United States Catholic Conference, 1995), no. 99.

46. Ibid.

47. *Evangelii Nuntiandi,* no. 58.

48. Chautard, *The Soul of the Apostolate,* 165.

49. John Paul II, *Christifideles Laici* (Boston: Pauline Books and Media, 1988), no. 23.

50. Ibid., no. 27.

51. Ibid., no. 30.

52. Benedict XVI, *Called to Communion,* 23.

53. United States Conference of Catholic Bishops, *National Directory For Catechesis* (Washington, DC: United States Conference of Catholic Bishops, 2005), 100.

54. Benedict XVI (Joseph Ratzinger), *Pilgrim Fellowship of Faith,* trans. Henry Taylor (San Francisco: Ignatius Press, 2002), 253.

55. John Paul II, *Novo Millennio Ineunte,* no. 48.

56. Benedict XVI (Joseph Ratzinger), *God and the World,* trans. Henry Taylor (San Francisco: Ignatius Press, 2000), 452–53.

57. Benedict XVI (Joseph Ratzinger), *Many Religions—One Covenant,* trans. Graham Harrison (San Francisco: Ignatius Press, 1999), 109–13.

58. John Paul II, *Redemptoris Missio,* no. 55.

59. United States Conference of Catholic Bishops, *Go and Make Disciples: A National Plan and Strategy for Catholic Evangelization in the United States* (Washington, DC: United States Conference of Catholic Bishops, 2001), no. 44.

60. John Paul II, "The Gospel Purifies Culture: Address to Representatives of Catholic Higher Education–Xavier University, New Orleans, September 12, 1987," in *John Paul II in America* (Boston: Daughters of St. Paul, 1987), 102.

61. *Redemptoris Missio,* no. 39.

62. Useful texts on this topic for religious educators include *Catholic Evangelization in an Ecumenical and Interreligious Society* (Washington, DC: United States Conference of Catholic Bishops, 2004) and two works by Francis Cardinal Arinze, *Religions for Peace: A Call for Solidarity to the Religions of the World* (New York: Doubleday, 2002), and *Meeting Other Believers: The Risks and Rewards of Interreligious Dialogue* (Huntington, IN: Our Sunday Visitor, 1998).

# Chapter V

1. Philip Hughes, *A History of the Church,* vol. 1 (New York: Sheed and Ward, 1949), 6–7.

2. John L. McKenzie, SJ, *Dictionary of the Bible* (New York: Macmillan Publishing Co., 1965), 53.

3. Fitzmyer, *The Acts of the Apostles,* 603.

4. Frederick Justus Knecht, *A Practical Commentary on Holy Scripture* (Rockford, IL: Tan Books and Publishers, 1993), 793. "A number of theological

writings are attributed to [Dionysius the Areopagite] by the Fathers and the medieval theologians, none of which are earlier than the 4th or 5th century AD" (McKenzie, *Dictionary of the Bible,* 199).

5. John Paul II, *Redemptoris Missio* (Boston: St. Paul Books and Media, 1990), no. 25.

6. Ibid.

7. Johnson, *The Acts of the Apostles,* 319.

8. John Paul II, Homily at the Olympic Centre of Athens, May 5, 2001, *L'Osservatore Romano,* May 9, 2001, 1.

9. Dawson, *The Formation of Christendom,* 148–49.

10. Note that today Christianity is the national religion of Greece.

11. H. Richard Niebuhr, *Christ and Culture* (New York: Harper Torchbooks, 1975), 194.

12. *Following Christ in Mission,* 112–14.

13. Buono, *Missiology,* 147.

14. John Paul II, Homily at the Olympic Center of Athens, May 5, 2001, 2.

15. Ibid.

16. John Paul II, Address to the Pontifical Council for Culture, March 16, 2002, *L'Osservatore Romano,* March 20, 2002, 2.

17. John Tracy Ellis, *John Lancaster Spalding* (Milwaukee: Bruce Publishing Company, 1961), 2.

18. David Francis Sweeney, OFM, *The Life of John Lancaster Spalding* (New York: Herder and Herder, 1965), 34.

19. Ellis, *John Lancaster Spalding,* 4.

20. Ibid.

21. Ibid., 11.

22. Robert N. Barger, *John Lancaster Spalding: Catholic Educator and Social Emissary* (New York: Garland Publishing, 1988), 176.

23. Merle Curti, *The Social Ideas of American Educators* (Totowa, NJ: Littlefield, Adams & Co., 1971), 354.

24. Barger, *John Lancaster Spalding,* 176.

25. Sweeney, *The Life of John Lancaster Spalding,* 127.

26. Curti, *The Social Ideas of American Educators,* 353–54.

27. Carey, *Catholics in America,* 223.

28. Ellis, *John Lancaster Spalding,* 36.

29. John Lancaster Spalding, *Means and Ends of Education* (Chicago: A. C. McClurg and Co., 1903), 224.

30. Ibid., 226–27.

31. Ellis, *John Lancaster Spalding,* 42–43.

32. Carey, *Catholics in America,* 55.

33. Curti, *The Social Ideas of American Educators,* 354.

34. Ibid.

35. Sweeney, *Life of John Lancaster Spalding,* 19.

36. Ibid.

37. Ibid., 67.

38. Ibid., 182–83.

39. John Paul II, Address to the Plenary Assembly of the Pontifical Council for Culture, *L'Osservatore Romano,* March, 20, 2002, 2.

40. John Paul II, *Crossing the Threshold of Hope,* 112–13.

41. Dawson, *The Historic Reality of Christian Culture,* 89.

42. Ibid., 90.

43. Ibid., 91.

44. Thomas E. Woods, *How the Catholic Church Built Western Civilization* (Washington, DC: Regnery Publishing, 2003).

45. Christopher Dawson, *The Crisis of Western Education* (New York: Sheed and Ward, 1961), 137–38.

46. Ibid., 136.

47. Ibid., 175.

48. Ibid., 201.

49. Ibid., 176.

50. Pontifical Council for Culture, *Towards A Pastoral Approach to Culture* (Washington, DC: United States Catholic Conference, 1999), no. 32.

51. Ibid.

52. Dawson, *The Historic Reality of Christian Culture,* 29.

53. Ibid., 29–30.

54. *General Directory For Catechesis*, no. 21.

55. Ibid., no. 203.

56. Ibid., no. 206.

57. Sources that can be useful to religious educators on the topic of inculturation include *The General Directory For Catechesis,* especially part IV, and *The National Directory for Catechesis,* especially chapter 2.

# Chapter VI

1. Craig S. Keener, *Matthew: The IVP New Testament Commentary Series,* ed. Grant R. Osborne (Downers Grove, IL: InterVarsity Press, 1997), 264–65.

2. William Barclay, *The Gospel of Matthew* (Louisville, KY: Westminster John Knox Press, 2001), 148.

3. Ibid.

4. Leo the Great, "A Homily on the Beatitudes, St. Matt. V. 1–9," in *Nicene and Post-Nicene Fathers,* vol. 12, ed. Philip Schaff and Henry Wace (Peabody, MA: Hendrickson Publishers, 1995), 202.

5. Rudolf Schnackenburg, *The Gospel of Matthew,* trans. Robert R. Barr (Grand Rapids, MI: Eerdmans Publishing Co., 2002), 151.

6. Ibid., 152.

7. Buono, *Missiology,* 94.

8. Woods, *How the Catholic Church Built Western Civilization,* 180.

9. Neill, *The History of Christian Missions,* 37–38.

10. Woods, *How the Catholic Church Built Western Civilization,* 175.

11. Benedict XVI, *Deus Caritas Est, Origins* 35, no. 33 (February 2, 2006): no. 22.

12. Ibid., no. 23.

13. Woods, *How the Catholic Church Built Western Civilization,* 176–79.

14. Benedict XVI, *Deus Caritas Est,* no. 40.

15. Mother Teresa, *No Greater Love,* ed. Becky Benenate and Joseph Durepos (Novato, CA: New World Library, 1997), 147.

16. Ibid., 151–52.

17. Sister M. Joseph, OP, *Out of Many Hearts* (Hawthorne, NY: The Servants of Relief for Incurable Cancer, 1965), 20.

18. Ibid., 20–21.

19. Ibid., 8.

20. *Rose Hawthorne Lathrop: Selected Writings,* ed. Diana Culberston, OP, Sources of American Spirituality Series (Mahwah, NJ: Paulist Press, 1993), 24–25.

21. Theodore Maynard, *A Fire Was Lighted: The Life of Rose Hawthorne Lathrop* (Milwaukee: Bruce Publishing Company, 1948), 229, 233–34.

22. Ibid., 250.

23. *Rose Hawthorne Lathrop: Selected Writings*, 50.

24. Boniface Hanley, OFM, "The More Things Change the More They Are the Same," *The Anthonian* 59 (2nd Quarter 1985): 12.

25. *Rose Hawthorne Lathrop: Selected Writings,* 50.

26. Ibid., 51.

27. Sister M. Joseph, OP, *Out of the Hearts of Many,* 25.

28. Ibid., 65.

29. Ibid., 66.

30. Maynard, *A Fire Was Lighted,* 329.

31. Sister M. Joseph, OP, *Out of Many Hearts,* 209.

32. Maynard, *Great Catholics*, 233.

33. Sister M. Joseph, OP, *Out of Many Hearts,* 196–204.

34. *Rose Hawthorne Lathrop: Selected Writings,* 51.

35. Ibid., 62.

36. Ibid., 56.

37. It often happens that the poorest are the most open and receptive to the words of the gospel.

38. Benedict XVI, *Deus Caritas Est,* no. 19.

39. Ibid., no. 25.

40. Paul VI, *Evangelii Nuntiandi,* no. 31.

41. Buono, *Missiology,* 147.

42. Rodger Charles, SJ, *An Introduction to Catholic Social Teaching* (San Francisco: Ignatius Press, 1999), 10.

43. Pontifical Council for Peace and Justice, *The Compendium of the Social Doctrine of the Church* (Libreria Editrice Vaticana, 2004), no. 63.

44. Ibid., no. 66.

45. Ibid.

46. John Paul II, *Memory and Identity* (New York: Rizzoli, 2005), 125.

47. Curt Cadorette, "Liberating Mission," in *Mission in Bold Humility: David Bosch's Work Considered,* ed. Willem Saayman and Klippies Kritzinger (Maryknoll, NY: Orbis Books, 1996), 65.

48. Benedict XVI, *Deus Caritas Est,* no. 31.

49. *Rose Hawthorne Lathrop: Selected Writings,* 189.

50. Benedict XVI, *Deus Caritas Est,* no. 31.

51. Ibid.

52. *Compendium of the Social Doctrine of the Church,* no. 529.

53. Ibid.

54. Benedict XVI, *Deus Caritas Est,* no. 28.

55. Ibid., no. 29.

56. Ibid., no. 28.

57. *Compendium of the Social Doctrine of the Church,* no. 531.

58. Benedict XVI, Message for Lent 2006: Jesus at the Sight of the Crowds, Was Moved With Pity, *L'Osservatore Romano,* February 8, 2006, 7. In addition to *Deus Caritas Est* and *The Compendium of the Social Doctrine of the Church,* religious educators may find Mother Teresa's *No Greater Love* to be useful as well.

59. See Ronald J. Sider, *Rich Christians in an Age of Hunger: Moving from Affluence to Generosity* (Nashville, TN: W Publishing Group, A division of Thomas Nelson Publishers, 1992), and Theodore Dalrymple, *Life at the Bottom: The Worldview That Makes the Underclass* (Chicago: Ivan R. Dee Publisher, 2001).

# Conclusion

1. Dulles, *Models of the Church,* 17.

2. Pontifical Council for Culture, *Towards a Pastoral Approach to Culture,* no. 27.

3. Benedict XVI (Joseph Ratzinger), "Culture and Truth," *Origins* 28, no. 36 (February 25, 1999): 628.

4. *Towards a Pastoral Approach to Culture,* no. 28.

5. John Paul II, Address in Sofia, Bulgaria, May 24, 2002, *L'Osservatore Romano,* May 29, 2002, 8.

6. Francis Arinze, "The Gospel in a Religiously Pluralistic World," *Origins* 29, no. 30 (January 13, 2000): 485.

7. Ibid.

8. Benedict XVI, "Culture and Truth," 628.

9. Walter Kasper, "Relating Christ's Universality to Interreligious Dialogue," *Origins* 30, no. 21 (November 2, 2000): 327.

10. Benedict XVI, "Christ, Faith and the Challenge of the Cultures," *Origins* 24, no. 41 (March 30, 1995): 683.

11. Ibid., 686.

12. Walter Kasper, *That They All May Be One* (New York: Burns and Oates, 2004), 39.

13. See *Redemption and Dialogue: Reading Redemptoris Missio and Dialogue and Proclamation,* ed. William R. Burrows (Maryknoll, NY: Orbis Books, 1994).

14. George Weigel, *Witness to Hope* (New York: HarperCollins Publishers, 1999), 9.

15. Ibid.

16. John Paul II, "To The Young Muslims of Morocco, Casablanca," August 19, 1985, in *Interreligious Dialogue: The Official Teaching of the Catholic Church from the Second Vatican Council to John Paul II,* ed. Francesco Gioia (Boston: Pauline Books and Media, 2006), 337.

17. Ibid., 343.

18. Ibid., 730.

19. Ibid.

20. John Paul II, Homily at Astana, Kazakhstan, September 23, 2001, *L'Osservatore Romano,* September 26, 2001, 1.

21. Ibid., 2.

22. John Paul II, *Ecclesia in America,* no. 74.

23. Perhaps this tension helps to explain the fact that globally, the evangelical church has a current annual growth rate of 4.7 percent and the Catholic

Church a rate of 0.5 percent. Generally speaking, evangelicals are not especially concerned about ecumenism. Consequently, their focus on evangelization is unencumbered by ecumenical considerations.

24. John Paul II, *L'Osservatore Romano,* July 3, 1996, nos. 3, 5.

25. Stephen J. Blaire "Catholic Evangelization in an Ecumenical and Interreligious Society," in *Catholic Evangelization in an Ecumenical and Interreligious Society* (Washington, DC: United States Conference of Catholic Bishops, 2004), 5.

26. Jeffrey Gros, Eamon McManus, and Ann Riggs, *Introduction to Ecumenism* (Mahwah, NJ: Paulist Press, 1998), 79.

27. *Unitatis Redintegratio,* no. 4, in *Vatican II.*

28. Ibid., no. 11.

29. Author's interview with Avery Cardinal Dulles, Fordham University, Fabor Hall, Room 255, June 24, 2004.

30. Stanley L. Jaki, *The Purpose of It All* (Port Huron, MI: Real View Books, 2005), 208.

31. Abbot Marmion, OSB, *Christ the Life of the Soul,* trans. a French Nun of Tyburn Convent (St. Louis, MO: B. Herder Book Co., 1925), 24.

32. Benedict XVI (Joseph Ratzinger), *Truth and Tolerance: Christian Belief and World Religions,* trans. Henry Taylor (San Francisco: Ignatius Press, 2004), 184.

33. *Lumen Gentium,* no. 8.

# BIBLIOGRAPHY

Antier, Jean-Jacques. *Charles de Foucauld.* Trans. Julia Shirek Smith. San Francisco: Ignatius Press, 1997.

Arinze, Francis Cardinal. *Meeting Other Believers: The Risks and Rewards of Interreligious Dialogue.* Huntington, IN: Our Sunday Visitor, 1998.

———. *Religions for Peace: A Call for Solidarity to the Religions of the World.* New York: Doubleday, 2002.

———. "The Gospel in a Religiously Pluralistic World." *Origins* 29, no. 30 (January 13, 2000).

St. Augustine. *The Confessions.* Trans. J. G. Pilkington. *Nicene and Post-Nicene Fathers,* vol. 1, edited y Philip Schaff. Peabody, MA: Hendrickson Publishers, 1995.

Aumann, Jordan. *Christian Spirituality in the Catholic Tradition.* San Francisco: Ignatius Press, 1986.

Avallone, Paul P., SDB. *Keys to the Hearts of Youth: St. John Bosco's Pastoral and Educational Mission, A Spirituality and Methodology.* New Rochelle, NY: Salesiana Publications, 1999.

Barclay, William. *The Gospel of Mark.* Louisville, KY: Westminster John Knox Press, 2001.

———. *The Gospel of Matthew.* Louisville, KY: Westminster John Knox Press, 2001.

Barger, Robert N. *John Lancaster Spalding: Catholic Educator and Social Emissary.* New York: Garland Publishing, 1988.

Benedict XVI. Angelus Address, October 23, 2005. *L'Osservatore Romano,* October 26, 2005.

———. Angelus Address, December 26, 2005. *L'Osservatore Romano,* January 4, 2006.

———. (Joseph Ratzinger) *Called to Communion.* Trans. Adrian Walker. San Francisco: Ignatius Press, 1996.

———. "Christ, Faith and the Challenge of the Cultures." *Origins* 24, no. 41 (March 30, 1995).

———. Christmas, The Council and Conversion in Christ, December 22, 2005. *L'Osservatore Romano,* January 4, 2006.

———. "Culture and Truth." *Origins* 28, no. 36 (February 25, 1999).

————. *Deus Caritas Est. Origins* 35, no. 33 (February 2, 2006).

————. (Joseph Ratzinger) *God and the World.* Trans. Henry Taylor. San Francisco: Ignatius Press, 2000.

————. (Joseph Ratzinger) *Many Religions—One Covenant.* Trans. Graham Harrison. San Francisco: Ignatius Press, 1999.

————. Message for Lent 2006: Jesus at the Sight of the Crowds, Was Moved With Pity. *L'Osservatore Romano,* February 8, 2006.

————. (Joseph Ratzinger), *A New Song for the Lord.* Trans. Martha M. Matesich. New York: Crossroad Publishing Company, 1997.

————. (Joseph Ratzinger) *Pilgrim Fellowship of Faith.* Trans. Henry Taylor. San Francisco: Ignatius Press, 2002.

————. (Joseph Ratzinger) *The Spirit of the Liturgy.* Trans. John Saward. San Francisco: Ignatius Press, 2000.

————. (Joseph Ratzinger) *Truth and Tolerance: Christian Belief and World Religions.* Trans. Henry Taylor. San Francisco: Ignatius Press, 2004.

————. *Without Roots.* Trans. Michael F. Moore. New York: Basic Books, 2006.

Berger, John A., CSSR. *Life of Right Rev. John N. Neumann, DD.* Trans. Eugene Grimm. New York: Benzinger Brothers, 1884.

Bishop's Committee on the Liturgy. *Environment and Art in Catholic Worship.* Washington, DC: United States Catholic Conference, 1978.

Bunson, Margaret R. *Kateri Tekakwitha: Mystic of the Wilderness.* Huntington, IN: Our Sunday Visitor, 1992.

Buono, Giuseppe. *Missiology: Theology and Praxis.* Nairobi: Paulines Publications Africa, 2002.

Butler, Jon, Grant Wacker, and Randall Balmer. *Religion in American Life: A Short History.* New York: Oxford University Press, 2003.

Cadorette, Curt. "Liberating Mission." In *Mission in Bold Humility: David Bosch's Work Considered,* edited by Willem Saayman and Klippies Kritzinger. Maryknoll, NY: Orbis Books, 1996.

Carey, Patrick W. *Catholics in America: A History.* Westport, CT: Praeger Publishers, 2004.

Carroll, Colleen. *The New Faithful: Why Young Adults Are Embracing Christian Orthodoxy.* Chicago: Loyola Press, 2002.

Carter, Stephen L. *The Culture of Disbelief: How American Law and Politics Trivialize Religious Devotion.* New York: Basic Books, 1993.

*Catechism of the Catholic Church.* San Francisco: Ignatius Press, 1994.

*Catholic Evangelization in an Ecumenical and Interreligious Society.* Washington, DC: United States Conference of Catholic Bishops, 2004.

Charles, Rodger, SJ. *An Introduction to Catholic Social Teaching.* San Francisco: Ignatius Press, 1999.

Chautard, Dom Jean-Baptiste, OCSO. *The Soul of the Apostolate.* Trans. Monk of Our Lady of Gethsemani. Trappist, KY: Abbey of Gethsemani, 1946.

Chinnici, Joseph P., OFM. *Living Stones: The History and Structure of Catholic Spiritual Life in the United States.* Maryknoll, NY: Orbis Books, 1996.

Chrysostom, St. John. "Homily on Acts, 17." In *The Navarre Bible, The Acts of the Apostles: Text and Commentaries.* Dublin: Four Courts Press, 1992.

Congregation for the Clergy. *General Directory For Catechesis.* Washington, DC: United States Catholic Conference, 1998.

Curley, Michael J., CSSR. *Bishop John Neumann.* Philadelphia: Bishop Neumann Center, 1952.

Curti, Merle. *The Social Ideas of American Educators.* Totowa, NJ: Littlefield, Adams & Co., 1971.

Dalrymple, Theodore. *Life At the Bottom: The Worldview That Makes the Underclass.* Chicago: Ivan R. Dee Publisher, 2001.

Dawson, Christopher. *The Crisis of Western Education.* New York: Sheed and Ward, 1961.

————. *Enquiries into Religion and Culture.* London: Sheed and Ward, 1934.

————. *The Formation of Christendom.* New York: Sheed and Ward, 1967.

————. *The Historic Reality of Christian Culture.* New York: Harper and Brothers Publishers, 1960.

————. *Religion and the Rise of Western Culture.* New York: Sheed and Ward, 1950.

de la Bedoyere, Michael. *The SaintMaker.* Manchester, NH: Sophia Institute Press, 1998.

De Murville, MNL Couvre. *The Man Who Founded California: The Life of Blessed Junipero Serra.* San Francisco: Ignatius Press, 2000.

De Sales, St. Francis. *The Introduction to the Devout Life.* Trans. John K. Ryan. New York: Doubleday, 1989.

*Documents of American Catholic History.* Ed. John Tracy Ellis. Milwaukee: Bruce Publishing Company, 1956.

Dolan, Jay P. *The American Catholic Experience.* Notre Dame, IN: University of Notre Dame Press, 1992.

————. *Catholic Revivalism: The American Experience 1830–1900.* Notre Dame, IN: University of Notre Dame Press, 1978.

Donahue, John R., and Daniel J. Harrington, SJ. *The Gospel of Mark.* Sacra Pagina Series, vol. 2, edited by Daniel J. Harrington, SJ. Collegeville, MN: Liturgical Press, 2002.

Bibliography

*Donum Veritatis.* Congregation for the Doctrine of the Faith (1990). In The Christian Faith in the Doctrinal Documents of the Catholic Church Series. Ed. Jacques Dupuis. New York: Alba House, 1995.

Dubay, Thomas. *The Evidential Power of Beauty.* San Francisco: Ignatius Press, 1999.

Dulles, Avery Cardinal. *Models of the Church.* New York: Image Books, 2002.

————. "The Rebirth of Apologetics." *First Things* 143 (May 2004).

Dupont, Jacques, OSB. "The Meal at Emmaus." In *The Eucharist in the New Testament: A Symposium.* Trans. E. M. Stewart. Baltimore: Helicon Press, 1965.

Eck, Diana L. *A New Religious America.* San Francisco: HarperCollins Publishers, 2001.

Ellis, John Tracey. *American Catholicism.* 2nd ed. Chicago: University of Chicago Press, 1969.

————. *Catholics in Colonial America.* Baltimore: Helicon Press, 1965.

————. *John Lancaster Spalding.* Milwaukee: Bruce Publishing Company, 1961.

*The Encyclopedia of American Catholic History.* Ed. Michael Glazier and Thomas J. Shelley. Collegeville, MN: Liturgical Press, 1997.

Fitzmyer, Joseph A. *The Acts of the Apostles.* The Anchor Bible, vol. 31. New York: Doubleday, 1998.

*Following Christ in Mission: A Foundation Course in Missiology.* Ed. Sebastian Karotemprel. Nairobi: Pauline Publications Africa, 1995.

Gallup, George H., and Wendy Plumb. *Scared: Growing Up In America.* Princeton: George H. Gallup International Institute, 1995.

Garesche, Edward F. *The Everyday Apostle: Commonsense Ways to Draw Others to Christ.* Manchester, NH: Sophia Institute Press, 2002.

Gaustad, Edwin, and Leigh Schmidt. *The Religious History of America.* San Francisco: HarperCollins Publishers, 2004.

Gibbs, Eddie. "Evangelization in the Catholic Church: An Evangelical Reflection." In *Evangelizing America,* edited by Thomas P. Rausch, SJ. Mahwah, NJ: Paulist Press, 2004.

————. "The Launching of Mission: The Outpouring of the Spirit at Pentecost." In *Mission in Acts: Ancient Narratives in Contemporary Context,* edited by Robert L. Gallagher and Paul Hertzig. Maryknoll, NY: Orbis Books, 2004.

Gould, Ezra P. *The Critical and Exegetical Commentary on the Gospel According to Saint Mark.* Edinburgh: T & T Clark, 1996.

Grace, Madeline. "Under Shadows of Death: The Spiritual Journey of Jean de Brebeuf and Isaac Jogues." *American Catholic Studies* 115, no. 3 (Fall 2004).

Gros, Jeffrey, Eamon McManus, and Ann Riggs. *Introduction to Ecumenism.* Mahwah, NJ: Paulist Press, 1998.

Guardini, Romano. *The Spirit of the Liturgy.* New York: Crossroad Publishing Company, 1998.

Hanley, Boniface, OFM. "The More Things Change the More They Are the Same." *The Anthonian* 59 (2nd Quarter 1985).

Hennesey, James, SJ. *American Catholics.* New York: Oxford University Press, 1983.

Holden, Vincent F., CSP. *The Yankee Paul: Isaac Thomas Hecker.* Milwaukee: Bruce Publishing Company, 1958.

Hughes, Philip. *A History of the Church.* Vol. 1. New York: Sheed and Ward, 1949.

*Interreligious Dialogue: The Official Teaching of the Catholic Church from the Second Vatican Council to John Paul II.* Ed. Francesco Gioia. Boston: Pauline Books and Media, 2006.

Jaki, Stanley L. *The Purpose of It All.* Port Huron, MI: Real View Books, 2005.

John Paul II. *Ad limina* Address to French Bishops, March 8, 1997. *L'Osservatore Romano,* March 19, 1997.

———. Address to the Plenary Assembly of the Pontifical Council for Culture. *L'Osservatore Romano,* March 20, 2002.

———. Address to the Pontifical Council for Culture, March 16, 2002. *L'Osservatore Romano,* March 20, 2002.

———. Address in Sofia, Bulgaria, May 24, 2002. *L'Osservatore Romano,* May 29, 2002.

———. *Catechesi Tradendae.* Boston: Daughters of St. Paul, 1980.

———. *Christifideles Laici.* Boston: Pauline Books and Media, 1988.

———. *Crossing the Threshold of Hope.* Ed. Vittorio Messori. New York: Alfred A. Knopf, 1994.

———. *Ecclesia de Eucharistia.* Boston: Pauline Books and Media, 2003.

———. "Ecclesia in America." *Origins* 28, no. 3 (February 4, 1999).

———. "The Gospel Purifies Culture: Address to Representatives of Catholic Higher Education—Xavier University, New Orleans, September 12, 1987." In *John Paul II in America.* Boston: Daughters of St. Paul, 1987.

———. Homily at Astana, Kazakhstan, September 23, 2001. *L'Osservatore Romano,* September 26, 2001.

———. Homily at the Olympic Centre of Athens, May 5, 2001. *L'Osservatore Romano,* May 9, 2001.

———. *Juvenum Patris.* Acts of The General Council of the Salesian Society of St. John Bosco. New Rochelle, NY: Salesian Communications, 1988.

———. "The Liturgy and Its Renewal." *Origins* 28, no. 21 (November 5, 1998).

———. *L'Osservatore Romano,* July 3, 1996.

———. *Memory and Identity.* New York: Rizzoli, 2005.

———. *Novo Millennio Ineunte.* Boston: St. Paul Books and Media, 2001.

————. *Redemptoris Hominis.* Washington, DC: United States Catholic Conference, 1979.

————. *Redemptoris Missio.* Boston: St. Paul Books and Media, 1991.

————. *Springtime of Evangelization: The Complete Texts of the Holy Father's 1998 Ad limina Addresses to the Bishops of the United States.* Ed. Thomas D. Williams, LC. San Francisco: Ignatius Press, 1999.

————. *Ut Unum Sint.* Washington, DC: United States Catholic Conference, 1995.

Johnson, Luke Timothy. *The Acts of the Apostles.* Sacra Pagina Series, vol. 5, edited by Daniel J. Harrington, SJ. Collegeville, MN: Liturgical Press, 1992.

Kasper, Cardinal Walter. "Relating Christ's Universality to Interreligious Dialogue." *Origins* 30, no. 21 (November 2, 2000).

————. *That They All May Be One.* New York: Burns and Oates, 2004.

Keener, Craig S. *Matthew: The IVP New Testament Commentary Series.* Ed. Grant R. Osborne. Downers Grove, IL: InterVarsity Press, 1997.

Kennedy, Malcolm M. "Evangelization and the Call to Holiness." In *The Church's Mission of Evangelization,* edited by William E. May. Steubenville, OH: Franciscan University Press, 1996.

Knecht, Frederick Justus. *A Practical Commentary on Holy Scripture.* Rockford, IL: Tan Books and Publishers, 1993.

Leo the Great. "A Homily on the Beatitudes, St. Matt. V. 1–9." In *Nicene and Post-Nicene Fathers,* vol. 12, edited by Philip Schaff and Henry Wace. Peabody, MA: Hendrickson Publishers, 1995.

Marmion, Abbot, OSB. *Christ the Life of the Soul.* Trans. a French Nun of Tyburn Convent. St. Louis, MO: B. Herder Book Co., 1925.

Maynard, Theodore. *A Fire Was Lighted: The Life of Rose Hawthorne Lathrop.* Milwaukee: Bruce Publishing Company, 1948.

————. *Great Catholics in American History.* Garden City, NY: Hanover House, 1957.

McKenzie, John L., SJ. *Dictionary of the Bible.* New York: Macmillan Publishing Co., 1965.

Merton, Thomas. "Conquistador, Tourist and Indian." In *Saints and Sinners,* edited by Greg Tobin. New York: Doubleday, 1999.

Morrison, John. *The Educational Philosophy of St. John Bosco.* New Rochelle, NY: Salesiana Publications, 1979.

Mother Teresa. *No Greater Love.* Ed. Becky Benenate and Joseph Durepos. Novato, CA: New World Library, 1997.

*National Directory for Catechesis.* Washington, DC: United States Conference of Catholic Bishops, 2005.

Neill, Stephen. *A History of Christian Missions.* New York: Penguin Books USA, 1990.

Neuhaus, Richard J. *The Naked Public Square.* Grand Rapids, MI: Eerdmans Publishing Co., 1984.

*The New American Bible.* Nashville, TN: Thomas Nelson Publishers, 1986.

Newman, John Henry Cardinal. *An Essay in Aid of a Grammar of Assent.* In *The Works of Cardinal Newman.* London: Longmans, Green, and Co., 1898.

Niebuhr, H. Richard. *Christ and Culture.* New York: Harper Torchbooks, 1975.

O'Brien, David J. *Isaac Hecker: An American Catholic.* Mahwah, NJ: Paulist Press, 1992.

O'Malley, Archbishop Sean. "Why Preaching Must Be a Priority Today." *Origins* 33, no. 45 (April 22, 2004).

Paul VI. *Evangelii Nuntiandi.* Boston: Daughters of St. Paul, 1976.

Pontifical Council for Culture. *Towards A Pastoral Approach to Culture.* Washington, DC: United States Catholic Conference, 1999.

Pontifical Council for Peace and Justice. *The Compendium of the Social Doctrine of the Church.* Libreria Editrice Vaticana, 2004.

Rainer, Thom S. *Surprising Insights From the Unchurched: And Proven Ways to Reach Them.* Grand Rapids, MI: Zondervan, 2001.

*Redemption and Dialogue: Reading Redemptoris Missio and Dialogue and Proclamation.* Ed. William R. Burrows. Maryknoll, NY: Orbis Books, 1994.

Robichaud, Paul, CSP. "Evangelizing America: Transformations in Paulist Mission." *US Catholic Historian* 2, no. 2 (Spring 1993).

*Rose Hawthorne Lathrop: Selected Writings.* Ed. Diana Culberston, OP. Sources of American Spirituality Series. Mahwah, NJ: Paulist Press, 1993.

Schnackenburg, Rudolf. *The Church in the New Testament.* Trans. W. J. O'Hara. New York: Seabury Press, 1965.

———. *The Gospel of Matthew.* Trans. Robert R. Barr. Grand Rapids, MI: Eerdmans Publishing Co., 2002.

Scott, Martin J., SJ. *Isaac Jogues: Missioner and Martyr.* New York: P. J. Kenedy and Sons, 1927.

Senn, Frank C. *The Witness of the Worshiping Community.* Mahwah, NJ: Paulist Press, 1993.

Shea, John Gilmary. *History of the Catholic Missions Among the Indian Tribes of the United States.* New York: P. J. Kenedy, 1881.

Sheen, Fulton J. *Peace of Soul.* New York: McGraw-Hill Book Company, 1949.

Sider, Ronald J. *Rich Christians in an Age of Hunger: Moving from Affluence to Generosity.* Nashville, TN: W Publishing Group, A division of Thomas Nelson Publishers, 1992.

Sister M. Joseph, OP. *Out of Many Hearts.* Hawthorne, NY: The Servants of Relief for Incurable Cancer, 1965.

Smith, David. *Mission After Christendom*. London: Darton, Longman and Todd, Ltd., 2003.

Soards, Marion L. *The Speeches in Acts:Their Content, Context and Concerns*. Louisville, KY: Westminster John Knox Press, 1994.

Spalding, John Lancaster. *Means and Ends of Education*. Chicago: A. C. McClurg and Co., 1903.

Sweeney, David Francis, OFM. *The Life of John Lancaster Spalding*. New York: Herder and Herder, 1965.

*The Teaching of the Twelve Apostles*. Trans. M. B. Riddle, DD. Ante-Nicene Fathers, vol. 7, edited by Alexander Roberts and James Donaldson. Peabody, MA: Hendrickson Publishers, 1995.

*A Testimony by St. Chantal*. Ed. Elizabeth Stopp. Hyattsville, MD: Institute of Salesian Studies, 1967.

Turks, Paul. *Philip Neri: The Fire of Joy*. Trans. Daniel Utrecht. Staten Island, NY: Alba House, 1995.

United States Conference of Catholic Bishops. *Go and Make Disciples: A National Plan and Strategy for Catholic Evangelization in the United States*. Washington, DC, 2001.

Urs von Balthasar, Hans. "The Grandeur of the Liturgy." *Communio International Catholic Review* 5, no. 4 (Winter 1978).

*Vatican Council II:The Conciliar and Post Conciliar Documents*. Ed. Austin Flannery, OP. Collegeville, MN: Liturgical Press, 1980.

Vecsey, Christopher. *On the Padres' Trail*. Notre Dame, IN: University of Notre Dame Press, 1996.

———. *The Paths of Kateri's Kin*. Notre Dame, IN: University of Notre Dame Press, 1997.

Weigel, George. *The Truth of Catholicism*. New York: HarperCollins Publishers, 2001.

———. *Witness to Hope*. New York: HarperCollins Publishers, 1999.

Woods, Thomas E. *How the Catholic Church Built Western Civilization*. Washington, DC: Regnery Publishing, 2003.

Wuerl, Bishop Donald. "A Look Inside the New U.S. Catechetical Directory." *Origins* 34, no. 33 (February 3, 2005).

161